PRAISE FOR
SELLING WITH A SERVANT HEART

"Jim Doyle challenged our companies. He challenged us to do it differently than our competitors. He showed us how to focus on our customers' needs before our own. Seventeen years of record-breaking results followed. Try it."

> Terry Hurley, President, Evening Post Industries

"As the CEO of a woman-owned consulting business, I understand that it is necessary to continuously grow our practice. Jim Doyle has written a book that aligns the sales process to our clients' needs and to the way that is most effective for us to develop long-term clients."

> Claire Fisher, Managing Principle/CEO, Change Capability, Inc.

"Many successful Hearst salespeople have employed the partnership approach to selling outlined in Selling with a Servant Heart. As someone who began my career in sales, I fully subscribe to Jim's philosophy; the best salespeople are fully vested in the success of the customer."

> Jordan Wertlieb, President, Hearst Television, Inc.

"As a minor league baseball franchise owner, I was at different times both a customer and a sales manager with a sales staff. Jim Doyle has crystallized the way I'd like to be sold to and has provided a great blueprint for developing successful salespeople."

> Frank Burke, former owner, Chattanooga Lookouts Baseball

"Making the bold move from selling to serving was transformational. After twenty years of selling, I've finally fallen in love with what I do. Jim's method resonates so well with me. This book is pivotal for anyone wanting to dramatically improve their career performance, but the best payoffs extend far beyond the professional realm."

> Lisa Rooks Morris, Top 1% producing agent, Premier Sotheby's
> International Realty

SELLING WITH A SERVANT HEART

www.amplifypublishing.com

Selling with a Servant Heart: Ten Lessons on the Path to Joy and Increased Income

For more information, please contact:
Amplify Publishing, an imprint of Mascot Books
620 Herndon Parkway #320
Herndon, VA 20170
info@amplifypublishing.com

Library of Congress Control Number: 2021910023

CPSIA Code: PRFRE0721A
ISBN-13: 978-1-63755-103-5

Printed in Canada

THIS BOOK IS DEDICATED TO ALL MY TEACHERS
AND MENTORS.

THANK YOU!

SELLING

with a

SERVANT HEART

Ten Lessons on the Path to Joy
and Increased Income

JIM DOYLE

amplify

TABLE OF CONTENTS

PART 3

PART 4

INTRODUCTION

I CAN TEACH YOU SEVENTEEN WAYS TO CLOSE A SALE.

I know a great technique for answering objections. Several, in fact.

But guess what? All of those wonderful sales techniques will have little to do with whether you'll find real success in sales. In fact, many of them may actually hurt your sales effectiveness.

Take closing. It's a skill featured in most sales training programs. But strong closing techniques may cost you more sales than they create. And yet lines like "Close early and close often" and "ABC ... Always be closing" are still so frequently used you'd think they are essential. To me, they describe selling that's seen as winning, as getting the customer's money. I hate that kind of selling. That kind of selling doesn't work. It absolutely won't bring you any real job satisfaction. And yet we still see people trying those approaches all the time. It's sad.

Let's face it. There are lots of negative perceptions about salespeople. Most are caused by people who were being "sold" by salespeople who believed all that "stuff." How many of us have had an experience with a "close early and close often" salesperson who made us feel like we needed a shower afterward? I can think of hundreds as I write this, and I am sure you can as well.

The simple truth? Much of what we sales trainers have taught for years simply doesn't work. Or better put, it has limited impact in today's sales environment.

What does work? That's what you'll discover in the pages of this book.

Make no mistake. This is a sales book. It's a book about achieving greater success and, yes, making more money in sales. It's not an accident that the first word in the title of this book is "selling." This is a book about selling. But it is about selling in a very different way.

For the last thirty years, I have been given an incredible gift. I have had the privilege of training and working with thousands of salespeople. I am guessing over twenty thousand salespeople have come through the training programs our company presents. I led most of those programs. These folks were *supposed* to learn from me. But as it turned out, I was the student. The real stars I've met became my teachers. What I have discovered is that these superstars come from a different place than most. Yes, they had drive. Huge amounts of drive. But their drive wasn't to just make a sale. Their drive was to make a difference in the lives of their customers. And they were totally convinced that when they did make a difference, they would be rewarded with huge success.

I came to believe that the drive to make a difference changed them. It led them to do business in ways that were not at all like most other salespeople. They had a way of working with customers that created massive amounts of differentiation. And yet, differentiation wasn't really their goal. But did it have impact. The biggest benefit? A huge percentage of repeat business that meant they didn't have to start over every quarter. These sellers developed lots of base business that stayed with them month after month and year after year.

When I started working on this book, I wanted to expand my research beyond the media industry in which I had spent most of my career. To do that, I've spent much of this last year interviewing some very successful salespeople in dozens of different industries. And guess what? These successful sellers have that same commitment to customers as the superstars in the media business. That commitment is way beyond being "customer focused." As one of these sellers told me, "I work for them. I want them to see me as someone who is a member of their team." They are putting the customer's needs in front of their own needs.

It works! It works so well that the success of some of the people you will meet in this book seems staggering.

Consider these sellers:

- An RV salesperson who probably does more dollar volume per year than anyone in the world. In fact, I'm pretty sure he personally sells more in dollar volume than 90 percent of the RV dealerships in America.

- A mortgage broker is considered a top performer if they do five to six closed mortgages per month. You'll meet someone who does six hundred each year. Ten times the volume of the top 5 percent producer.

- A management consultant who routinely sold six- and seven-figure consulting deals to major companies when she was still in her twenties.

And so many more.

I have been inspired by the salespeople I have met putting together this book. They are my newest teachers.

I took what I learned from these teachers and combined that with the lessons from my own sales journey. They give us a road map. A road map with specific things you can do to serve your customers more effectively and have your customers quickly notice the difference. The ten lessons in this book turn what I have learned from these smart teachers into things you can immediately do to become more successful.

My goal as I write this book is to have you come to believe that trusting your instincts to serve can produce massive results and that, as you change your selling approach to embrace that desire to serve, you'll find huge success.

I call this way of selling "Selling with a Servant Heart." And when you sell like these teachers do, you will find more success than you could ever imagine.

And your sales job will bring you a lot more joy.

JIM DOYLE
SARASOTA, FLORIDA
JUNE 2021

PART I

WHAT IS SELLING WITH A SERVANT HEART?

"A TRUE SERVANT SALESPERSON, TO ME, IS NOT ATTACHED TO THE OUTCOME OF THE SALE. WHAT THEY'RE ATTACHED TO IS THE BEST INTEREST OF THE PERSON THEY'RE TALKING TO." —OSCAR MEJIA

OSCAR MEJIA CAME TO AMERICA FROM HONDURAS IN 1990 WHEN HE WAS TWENTY-SEVEN YEARS OLD. When he arrived in Texas, he couldn't speak English. In Honduras, he had fallen in love with being on the radio during college. Soon after coming to Texas, he started working for a Spanish language radio station and finally convinced management to let him have a shot at sales.

Today, some thirty years later, Oscar is one of the most successful advertising salespeople in America. He calls on clients for Univision in Dallas. Yes, Oscar makes a lot of money, and he's proud of his success. But what people who know Oscar will tell you is his loyalty from customers is beyond rare. Every salesperson has churn—customers who don't return. No exceptions. But Oscar's churn is so low that he has a huge base of business that grows every year.

But low churn isn't the secret to Oscar's success. The "secret" is how obsessed he is with his customers getting impact from what he sells them. Oscar says, "I work for them. I want my customers to think I am their employee." If you happen to be in Dallas at a promotional event involving Univision and one of Oscar's clients, you might find him in the parking lot picking up litter or bringing shopping carts back to the store entrance.

He's obsessed. Obsessed to create impact for his customers. That is how he serves them. And that customer obsession causes Oscar's client churn to be so incredibly low. That's why he has the success that he has had.

Take a second to think about how churn impacts your business. Many salespeople have ongoing relationships with their customers. Some customers leave every year. That's called churn. And every salesperson has some. But what happens if you can reduce your churn? The math is simple. When you have incredibly high repeat business, you start each year or quarter with a huge advantage over other salespeople.

My teachers who are Servant Heart Sellers love to sell! And they are good at it. But they will tell you that the real secret to their success is that obsessive focus on customer outcomes. That is what leads to loyalty. Their customers see how these sellers are obsessed with wanting to help them. And the customers respond! Oscar's customers love him! But what they really love is the impact on their business of what he sells, plus his ability to give them good advice. Even though Servant Heart Sellers have incredibly positive relationships, sellers like Oscar never forget why customers give them money. They know customers don't do that out of friendship. It is all about results.

This is an important point. Everyone likes great relationships. And some sellers believe that's the path to success. But Servant Heart Sellers would disagree. They know their job is to make a difference for their customers, not just to be their friend.

Most salespeople have *way* more churn than they could have. But as you get more consistent in practicing the principles outlined in this book, your churn will drop. And your sales and income will go up because of it.

Dave Wall works for Liberty Coach. He sells those big luxury motorhomes you occasionally see on the road. These rigs can cost as much as $2 million each! He sells a bunch of them every year, both new and pre-owned. With those prices, he probably does more sales volume than most RV dealerships do. That surely impresses me. Dave's customers are demanding. They are usually wealthy entrepreneurs who have sold a business or decided to switch from a sixty-foot-long boat to a fancy forty-five-foot-long motor coach.

A total of 60 percent of Dave's customers are repeat—60 percent! In a typical year, another 30 percent of his customers are referred by his previous buyers. When 90 percent of your business is repeat and referral, prospecting gets easy, eh? The person who told me about Dave is a tough buyer (I know . . . he was my client for years!). And he went on and on about how committed Dave was to his customers. Need an example? My friend had a question about something to do with his coach. He called Dave's cell. As they were talking, my friend asked

Dave where he was. And it turned out that he was on vacation in Argentina. You might think it is crazy to be answering routine questions from a customer on a satellite phone in South America. But Dave told me he thinks that doing little things like that—taking just five minutes to help—is the reason that he has been successful.

Does that level of commitment to his customers pay off? How would you answer that? It won't be a surprise that Dave has some customers who have bought eight or nine big coaches from him. He has built incredible loyalty because he is obsessed with serving his customers. And his customers become his best salespeople.

And by the way, the coaches Dave sells are by far the most expensive coaches out there. Often $400,000–$500,000 higher than his competitors.

THIS IS *WAY* BEYOND BEING CUSTOMER FOCUSED.

Most salespeople would be considered to be product focused by their customers. They can be like peddlers riding from town to town selling "stuff." That means their primary focus is on closing a sale. Their thinking tends to be pretty short term. They want to get the next deal done.

A smaller percentage of salespeople are seen by their customers as being customer focused. The critical words in that last sentence? Seen by their customers. Many, many sellers think they are customer focused, but if their customers don't see them that way, it really won't make a difference. Customer-focused sellers are less focused on the next sale and more focused on the account. Because of that, they think long term, thinking about what is good for the account.

I respect customer-focused salespeople. Many are hugely successful. But this is a book about a level of customer engagement that is way beyond being customer focused. The people I interviewed for this book are probably in the top 2 to 3 percent of all salespeople. These selling stars are obsessed with customer outcomes. Those sellers are truly seen as business partners by their clients. Their goal is to be seen by their clients as an unpaid member of the client's team.

Servant Heart Sellers have a set of actions that intentionally set them apart from their competition. They create incredible customer loyalty that drives their success. Some of these sellers have strictly business relationships with their customers. Others have clients who have become friends. But friendship, while wonderful, is *not* the goal. These sellers' motivation is not the relationship. It's providing the outcome the customer is looking for by buying or using what they sell. If we become friends, some of these sellers would say that's okay. But it's a by-product of the work we do . . . not the goal.

And guess what? These sellers, as you would expect, are givers. No one I approached for an interview turned me down. They have willingly and completely shared the secrets of their success in their interviews. Those lessons are the basis for the selling approach this book outlines.

Could you have that kind of success?

As you'll read, many of the sellers profiled here weren't always Servant Heart Sellers. That's certainly my personal story. Some told me that selling this way wasn't their natural way to do it. One shared that he had to make a transition from transactional, "get the order" selling to a long-term approach where he became obsessed with the customer outcomes.

They grew, over time, into this way of selling. And as they embraced these principles, their income went up, and the satisfaction they felt about their career soared.

Does Servant Heart Selling Work?

When Justin Gurney worked for the National Basketball Association, he had a bird's-eye seat to how the thirty NBA teams (and hundreds of salespeople) handled their ticket sales process. How did he get that view? He was their consultant, hired by the NBA to help teams grow sales and share best practices.

Justin told me that the typical sales approach for major league sports teams was to make one hundred phone calls a day. This is a selling approach now aided by technology to make sure the calls are more frequently going to people who may have engaged with the team's website or opened an email.

"Make more sales calls" is a common sales management instruction. I've sure encouraged that a few times when I was a sales manager. Many managers preach that. I was convinced that activity drove performance. But think about this. If more calls are done badly, all that drives is frustration, burnout, and high sales staff churn.

In his work, Justin discovered something powerful. On almost every NBA team's sales staff were one or two outliers. They had a different approach, one focused on building long-term relationships and discovering the business reasons driving a customer's purchase of NBA game tickets or entertainment packages. And guess who the most successful sellers were? The ones who did it differently!

As you read about the incredible salespeople whose ideas have formed this book, I am positive you'll come to believe that this is a way of selling that can have serious impact on your income and job satisfaction.

Are You New to Sales?

Zig Ziglar may have been the biggest name in motivational speaking for over forty years until his passing in 2012. Among the many famous quotes Zig was known for, one really describes the message of this book: "You can have everything in life you want if you will just help other people get what they want."

Your success in sales, likely your success in life, will be a function of how much you serve others.

If you are new to selling, you'll get a lot of advice. You'll get direction from your bosses. Your new colleagues will try to be helpful.

Much of the advice pays forward the way your bosses or colleagues were trained: "Make more calls. Sales is a numbers game. The more people you ask, the more sales you'll close."

Much of the advice you'll receive has validity. You do have to work hard to find success in sales. But making a lot of bad calls isn't going to bring you the success you deserve.

But when you sell with Zig Ziglar's advice in mind, that's when it gets magical.

Jeff Wagner is one of the most successful mortgage brokers in America. The average mortgage broker may close two to three loans per month. Jeff closes thirty or more. He tells every prospective customer, "My goal for this call and for this relationship is to give you the best advice possible, even if you chose to do your mortgage with someone else." Help them get what they want, and you will win.

AJ Vaden, cofounder and CEO of Brand Builders Group, found huge success selling six-figure consulting projects while she was still in her twenties. She describes selling with a Servant Heart like this: "It's selling without my needs in mind. It's not about what's going to earn me the most commissions or accolades. It's about your ability to put someone else's needs above your own."

Yes. Make a lot of calls. But make them with a Servant Heart, and you'll find huge success in your new sales career.

NOT YOUR TYPICAL
SALES BOOK

HERE'S AN EXERCISE. Look at any list of books about sales and check out their titles. Many of those titles reflect a way of selling that is the opposite of what is advocated in this book.

The words in the titles of those books tell you so much about what the writers believe. Closing, pitch, mastering, challenging, persuading, and—my favorite (note sarcasm here)—*winning*.

I suspect each of those books has ideas that can help someone get better. After all, maybe you need to know what a "tie down" or an "inverted tie down" is. If you're curious, those are forms of trial closing. Maybe that's helpful to know. But I am pretty sure the sales stars interviewed for this book have no clue what they mean.

I hate so many of the words in the titles of those selling books. They describe selling in a way that is contrary to everything I believe. Selling is not about winning. Sports teams win.

And when they win, that means another team has lost. Sales-people who view selling as winning might make sales, but they'll have little loyalty and a lot more churn. Read that phrase again: little loyalty and a lot more churn.

Here's an example. I wish this wasn't common, but sadly it is. A few years ago, I was in a meeting with a sales manager at a car dealership. A very excited salesperson came in to tell him that he had closed a sale with a mega-huge gross profit. Most car salespeople are paid on that profit, so the salesperson was pumped. The manager's response while high-fiving? "You put him to sleep!" This is another way of saying, "Congratulations on screwing that customer." I hate that. I can't begin to tell you how much I hate that. Stop celebrating that kind of talk.

Maybe that kind of selling works for some people. It must because a lot of salespeople have been doing that for a long time. But it is not the path to long-term success. And it certainly won't bring you much joy. Imagine going home tonight and telling your partner, "I put a customer to sleep today. Let's get dressed up and go out to celebrate." Selling is not about winning. Selling is about serving. And the more you serve, the more success you will have. Period.

Make no mistake. Every salesperson profiled in this book likes to close sales. I have been selling more than fifty years, longer if you count the annual Boy Scout candy sale. And I still get excited every time a prospect says yes. I am always aware of when it's the time in my presentation to ask for the sale. You'll see that sellers in this book are also aware of that. They want to get a commitment. What's the difference? Their path to success is based on being of maximum service to their customers. That motivates them as much—or more—than just "winning" a sale.

Like most successful salespeople, they are also incredibly competitive. That's me, for sure. While starting the research for this book, I picked the brain of a friend who launched a very successful sales book in 2020. He told me how many copies he had sold in the first ninety days. And I instantly became obsessed with selling more. I had not written a single word of the book at that point, but I wanted to sell more books than my friend. If you are reading this, thank you for helping. Only a few thousand more need to be sold in order for me to "win!"

So yes. Most great sellers are competitive. But when it comes to customers, Servant Heart Sellers don't focus much on what a win looks like for them. They are *always* focused on what winning looks like for their customers. This turns out to be what really creates success for the seller.

The Danger of Ego Drive

For years, I used the Caliper Profile as part of a prescreening for sales applicants. One of the key success elements they measured was called ego drive, which they defined as a strong desire to win. They also looked at empathy because when highly empathetic people also have huge drive, that's a strong predictor of success.

There's a very thin line between ego drive and egotism. Google defines egotism this way: "excessively conceited or absorbed in oneself; self-centered." When ego drive turns into egotism, lots of things change.

When egotistical people get into sales, their desire to win is stronger than anything else. If the customer wins, they are okay with that, but they don't really care. It's about them. They win because that's their self-image. Usually egotism is a function of huge insecurity. They have to win to make themselves feel better. Lots of salespeople have that. It's when winning becomes more important than serving that the ego starts to hurt, not help, the long-term performance of the salesperson.

You'll meet lots and lots of salespeople who are egotistical. And if their drive is high, they might get some results. They are so driven that they can win on that alone. But it's tough for egotistical people to form connections. And if you don't form connections, you have little chance at being a Servant Heart Seller.

Humility as a Sales Word

As I conducted interviews for this book, it was amazing how often the word "humility" showed up. For Shamire Goodwin, who sells advertising for WISN TV in Milwaukee, it means not thinking you know everything. He says, "For me, humility means there's still so much for me to do and to learn." For Landmark National Bank's Dean Thibault, humility can sometimes mean acknowledging when they are not a fit. He says, "We can't take care of everybody, but we know what we can deliver and what we're all about. For those clients who see the value in it, it's a long-term relationship that doesn't break."

Those comments suggest a big difference from someone so driven to make a sale that they don't care much about fit. And very different from the big-ego seller who thinks (or at least acts) like they know everything.

You may know the name Patrick Lencioni. His book *The Five Dysfunctions of a Team* is a must read for leaders. But he has another book that I have given away dozens of times. It's called *The Ideal Team Player*. In that book, he outlines three characteristics of the people organizations need to attract. And the first attribute is "humble." Yes, humility is a sales word.

Lencioni acknowledges two other attributes. The people who are great team players are hungry; they do want to win. And they are what he calls smart, which isn't book smart, but rather, people who have what I might call "situational awareness." They can see the clues about how their behavior might impact others. I'm not sure Lencioni is saying that any one is more important than the other two. I am guessing most Servant Heart Sellers have all three. But it's clear from my interviews with them that they certainly have humility. As you look at the lessons in this book, it might be that humility is at the foundation of all of them.

The Servant Heart Sellers' Difference

There are ten lessons outlined in this book based on the interviews with Servant Heart Sellers. After each lesson, look for the section called "The Servant Heart Sellers' Difference." In this section, you'll see the contrast between the lesson that's been presented and how many salespeople act. Read this section carefully. If you are like me, some of these "not-so-good behaviors" sometimes will show up in your approach to business. The people interviewed for this book would be the first to tell you they don't practice every one of the ten lessons perfectly or consistently. Being able to compare where you are today with the approach laid out in the lessons will give you a clear road map for change.

THIS WAS NOT MY DEFAULT

THERE WAS A COMMON THEME IN THE INTERVIEWS FOR THIS BOOK. Many of these great sellers confessed that selling with this commitment to the customer was *not* their natural way. For many, it was an approach they evolved into overtime.

Rory Vaden is a powerful speaker and author of the *New York Times* bestseller *Take the Stairs*. We've been colleagues in the National Speakers Association for a long time. When a friend suggested he'd be a great interview for this book, I was excited. So imagine my surprise when he said, "Today, I am an ambassador of Servant Heart Selling. But it's not something that comes naturally to me. I am self-centered naturally."

Rory has had an incredibly successful career. He said, "I am extremely competitive and hard driving. So when I first started in sales, that's how I approached it. That's how I was trained. Always be closing . . . don't leave till they buy." Like many sellers, Rory was taught that the customer had "his money, and his goal was to get the cash."

At some point, Rory had an experience that also happened to me on my sales journey. The mindset changes from one of scarcity—there's not enough—to one of abundance. Abundance is the belief that there is plenty for both of us. When I have an abundance mindset, I start looking for opportunities for others to win. Rory and the others profiled here go way beyond what is called win-win selling. Win-win selling suggests that I want to win, and I want my customer to win, as well. When you focus on win-win selling, you still have a motivation to win yourself. But Servant Heart Sellers take that further. Their primary motivation is for the customer to win. They truly believe that if the customer wins, they will be well taken care of. That's the selling approach that Rory embraces today. And the impact on his business has been huge.

For many salespeople, it takes time, and perhaps some success, to grow into this approach to sales. WBAL-TV's Barbara Anderson has had a very successful career in sales and sales management. Her corporate bosses suggested I interview her, which is the ultimate compliment. I am certain lots of people can identify with how Barbara describes her path:

> When I started, I was afraid to be myself. I remember I was probably twenty-eight years old, and I'd been in accounting. I remember sitting at my desk, and I would listen to the guy next to me, and he was funny. So I thought, *That's how you sell . . . you're funny.* But I wasn't funny. Then someone else was very analytical, and I go, "I'm just going to study the numbers and really be analytical." But that didn't work for me either. So I kept going around the office trying to be like someone

else. Finally, I thought to myself, *None of these really fit.* I made a lot of mistakes when I started, and I found out after a while that people appreciated when I would say, "I don't know. I'm not sure. I made a mistake." I think being humble was easier than trying to make things up as I went along and pretending about something I didn't know.

There's a long-running debate about how much people are capable of changing. People ask if the leopard ever changes its spots. And maybe what Rory and others describe is not a fundamental 180-degree change but rather a behavior that evolves. Management coach Peter McCampbell believes we don't change our spots, but we do have learned behavior. He says, "The simplest example is this. Like almost everybody else, I burned their hand on a hot stove as a kid. Why? Because I was curious. After that, I learned to wave my hand over, checking for heat. It didn't stop my curiosity. I had to learn behavior on whether I touch the stove."

If you have a strong drive to succeed and you are smart enough to pay attention to clues about how your behavior needs to change, you will likely figure out when something is not working. That's learned behavior. As Peter McCampbell says, "If you get thrown out of someplace for being too aggressive, you'll do a post analysis and hopefully say, 'I better not do that again.'"

Every person interviewed for this book has a strong drive to be successful. Most of you who are reading have that drive as well. It can frequently take time to start using that drive in a way that feels right for you and is consistent with your values. And sometimes it takes a while to determine what those values really are. The sellers in this book would tell you that they are different today than they were at the beginning of their careers. They have developed a sales approach that works for them and that has led them to greater success.

Scarcity Mentality vs. Abundance Mentality

What is a scarcity mentality? Blogger Grayson Bell says, "It is the belief that there will never be enough—whether it's money, food, emotions, or something else entirely—and as a result, your actions and thought stem from a place of lack. Instead of believing that you have enough and there is plenty to go around, you cling to everything you have out of fear of coming up short."

When I reflect back on the earliest years of my career, I am guessing a scarcity mentality was one of my driving forces. I was focused on winning. I liked it when the customer won, but it certainly wasn't my primary motivation. I had success. But I wasn't as fulfilled as I became when my thinking evolved to believing that there was enough for everyone. You could win, the colleagues on my team could win, and there would still be more than enough for me.

People with an abundance mindset connect with the idea that everything we send out into the world comes back. So if we offer love, service, and even money to others, we will get back love, money, and service from others. But the opposite is also true. If I offer sarcasm, judgment, and a sense of lack to the world, that is what I will get back. The more people cultivate an abundance mindset, the easier it is to work for the win for the other person. That's foundational to Servant Heart Selling.

Men Who Sell!

I found this 1950s sales training program, Men Who Sell, in the basement of a radio station I ran years ago. Apparently, it got sent to subscribers every month. Every time I look at it, I laugh because many of the greatest sellers I've met in the last thirty years have been women. And women may be more able to intuitively adopt the principles outlined in this book.

Men may start with a disadvantage when it comes to being a Servant Heart Seller. The testosterone-fueled instinct for fight or flight gets in the way of men learning to sell this way. Behavioral Essentials founder Rick Breden believes that for highly ambitious young men, in particular, being of service to others is not likely their highest priority. He says, "Hopefully we get to a point of maturity. Usually it's around age forty-five or so where there's more reflection. There's more, 'What am I really doing, and what really satisfies?' If you make that inquiry at any level of depth and consistency, there has to be some part of it that's giving back."

And so change begins.

The consulting firm ZS did assessment of salespeople in different industries, including financial services, industrial services, and health care. They studied seven different attributes. Both men and women used all seven to some extent. But high-performing women were more likely to emphasize connecting, shaping solutions, and collaborating. High-performing men? They relied more on improving and driving outcomes. Driving outcomes? Just that term sounds like a selling approach that is "testosterone fueled."

So can you change? *Yes.* Change requires willingness and awareness. But know this. All change is evolutionary. We may not do something perfectly at first. But if you have the willingness to change and a belief that there is a better path, you are well on your way.

The Bottom Line

You may not naturally be a Servant Heart Seller. That's pretty common. And it's okay. Don't spend even a second worrying about that. Chances are you didn't pick this book up by accident. I'm betting you have an instinct to serve, and you like seeing other people do well. If that describes you, then you can accelerate your growth and your success by putting the lessons from our teachers into practice.

PART II

WHAT'S IN IT FOR *YOU*?

WE'VE BEEN TAUGHT THAT EVERY SALES PRESENTATION SHOULD ANSWER THE BUYERS WIIFM QUESTION. WIIFM—What's in it for me?

This book wants to make a sale to you. I am hoping you will start to believe that there is a different way to approach sales.

Here are ten things that can happen for you if you adopt this way to sell—the answer to the WIIFM question:

1. You will make more money by selling this way. A lot more!

2. You will find more joy in your professional life. When you stop trying to close a sale and start focusing on making a difference, selling becomes a whole lot less stressful and a lot more fulfilling.

3. You'll have lower client churn. Imagine keeping customers longer and the impact that would have on your business.

4. Your closing percentage will go up. A lot! That will increase the impact of the hours you work. You might even be able to work fewer hours.

5. Your relationship with your customers will change. They will see you as a trusted business partner. And some will become your friends. That's not the goal, but it can be a nice added benefit.

6. You will have more opportunities for business with existing customers. And that's always easier business to work than finding completely new prospects. You'll get that because they trust you.

7. You will have opportunities to truly make a difference for your clients. Servant Heart Sellers are focused on either solving client problems or helping them achieve growth for their businesses. And when they accomplish that, they find a real sense of fulfillment.

8. You will be seen as very different from your competitor because this selling approach is so rare.

9. Your selling will become fun.

10. You will gain more money and greater joy when you make the transition to Servant Heart Selling.

THE TEN LESSONS FROM SERVANT HEART SELLERS

LET'S MEET OUR TEACHERS.

I have been selling for almost fifty years. During the last thirty years, I've also been a sales trainer, and I've met thousands and thousands of sellers. Plus, our JDA consultant group makes more than four thousand sales calls each year. All of that experience has influenced this book. But I wanted more. Most of my professional experience is with people who sell advertising. And I wanted to see how these ideas worked in other industries. Before I started to write, I sought to interview people from a variety of different businesses. All of them practice the ideas this book lays out. All are very successful. They are the best of the best. And their ideas and insights about the way they do business have shaped this book in very significant ways.

Because you'll hear so much from them in the pages of this book, I wanted to introduce them to you now and give you a little background about their experience. These people have inspired me!

Barbara Anderson—General Sales Manager, WBAL-TV in Baltimore.

Rick Breden—Founder of Behavioral Essentials (www.behavorialessentials.com). Rick, a psychotherapist by training, helps companies screen applicants and coaches leaders on how to build high-performing teams.

Pierre Bouvard—Currently Chief Insights Officer at Westwood One. Pierre is the only seller on this list who has actually called on me. That was when he was working for Arbitron, a company that provided ratings for radio stations. He later became president of sales and marketing at Arbitron.

Albert Fox, CFP, CIMA—Albert is a founding member of the Fox, Penberthy & Dehn Group at Morgan Stanley outside Philadelphia. They serve high net-worth clients.

Bill Gangloff—Senior Account Executive at WYFF TV. He is a multiple winner of Hearst Eagle Award recognizing sales performance. He's been with WYFF for over thirty years.

Shamire Goodwin—Senior Account Executive at Hearst, Milwaukee. He is also a multi-year Eagle Award winner during his seventeen-year tenure at WISN.

Justin Gurney—When I interviewed Justin, he was overseeing premium sales as Senior Vice President of the New Jersey Devils hockey team. Prior to this, he helped the thirty-two NBA teams grow revenue from ticket sales as Associate VP of the NBA.

Rhonda Kuhlman—Senior Account Executive at Hearst, Orlando. She is a frequent winner of her company's highest annual sales recognition.

Meg Linne—Meg is a National Account Manager for PepsiCo. She has only one account, which is one of the largest retailers in America.

Randy Mascagni, CFP—Randy operates Mascagni Wealth Management in Clinton, Mississippi.

Peter McCampbell—Chief Talent Officer and owner of Human Capital Metrics. Peter helps companies find, improve, and lead talent.

Jim McIngvale, aka Mattress Mac—Mattress Mac owns Gallery Furniture in Houston, considered by many as the most successful furniture store in America.

Oscar Mejia—Account Executive, Univision, Dallas. He is perhaps one of the most successful media sales reps I have ever met.

David Melville—Senior Consultant at JDA.media since 2005.

Jasmine Ruschmann—Regional sales manager at RXBAR, Chicago.

Brian Richmond—Vice President, Richmond Agency. He is an independent insurance agent and health benefit consultant in Jackson, Michigan.

Jim Stoos—A former client of Jim Doyle and Associates and now a Senior Marketing Consultant for our company.

Dean Thibault—Executive Vice President, Landmark National Bank. Dean oversees the commercial banking team for Landmark's offices throughout Kansas.

AJ Vaden—AJ is the Cofounder and CEO of Brand Builders, a personal brand strategy firm. Prior to founding Brand Builders, she served Southwestern Consulting, handling business development, coaching, and training.

Rory Vaden—Author of the *New York Times* bestselling book *Take the Stairs*. He's a member of the National Speakers Association Hall of Fame and Cofounder of Brand Builders.

Mike VandDevere—Mike is President of the family-owned VanDevere dealerships. They operate a Chevrolet, Cadillac, and Kia store in Akron, Ohio.

Jeff Wagner—Located in Houston, Jeff may be one of the most successful mortgage brokers in America. He serves as National Vice President of OneTrust Home Loans.

Dave Wall—Dave sells very expensive luxury motor coaches for Liberty Coach, and in partnership with Liberty, he owns the Motor Home Exchange, a used coach dealership.

Randy Watson—A long-term teacher of mine, Randy is now retired from WTHR-TV in Indianapolis.

I WORK FOR THEM

I TELL PEOPLE TO BE BIG PIE PEOPLE RATHER THAN
SMALL PIE PEOPLE. SMALL PIE PEOPLE SAY, "HOW DO I
GET MY PIECE OF THE PIE? IF I DON'T GET MY PIECE OF
THE PIE, I MAY NOT GET ENOUGH." BIG PIE PEOPLE SAY,
"THERE'S PLENTY OF PIE OUT THERE, SO WHEN I HELP
YOU GET YOUR PIECE, I'LL GET MY PIECE." WE HAVE TO BE
BIG PIE-MINDED PEOPLE. —MIKE VANDEVERE

"I WORK FOR THEM." That's a profoundly different attitude than thinking that I "sold" this customer or I "call on" this client. And yet that message—I work for them—was one of the consistent ideas from so many of the people interviewed for this book.

Shamire Goodwin is very clear about that. "You're a team-mate with your clients," he says. "You work for them. That's why I call them my bosses. You're on their team. You must think of yourself as an employee for each business that you work for. It's imperative that you see yourself in that role."

That obviously starts with the mindset of service. And it is so consistent with Zig Ziglar's belief that "You can have everything in life you want, if you will just help other people get what they want."

This is *way* beyond being customer focused.

When the great speaker and trainer Don Beveridge would speak to salespeople, he could be very tough. He'd tell them he thought most sellers, upward of 90 percent, were seen by their customers as being product focused. Beveridge called them peddlers. Peddlers sell stuff. Beveridge also believed that *only* 7 to 8 percent of all salespeople would be seen by their clients as customer focused. But as we mentioned earlier, there's a level of selling *way* beyond being customer focused. That's what's described in this book. That's when you are seen by your customer as an unpaid member of their team. Beveridge would say that's when you are seen as a partner with your customers.

A partner, not a vendor. Sounds like a great phrase. But those aren't just words for Servant Heart Sellers. They work to demonstrate customer partnership with all their actions.

Here's a powerful example. Think about the company or agent you buy your home insurance from. Like you, I've bought insurance for my cars, houses, and toys for years. In fact, I just paid for the renewal of a policy for our cottage a few days ago. I bought that insurance policy twelve years ago when I bought the cottage. And I have never heard from the agent again. I couldn't even tell you their name. My only contact with that company is the bill that came last week to renew the policy. Does that sound similar to your experience? Truth be told, I don't think I have ever heard from any agent about any insurance renewal in my life. Never! I've called them to add a new car or cancel a homeowner's policy after a sale. But a call from them? That has never happened.

That's why I was blown away when Brian Richmond told me about their approach to customers at the Richmond Agency. Brian is a Servant Heart Seller for sure. He's taken those principles not only to the business customers he serves but also to every client of their agency.

Almost every independent insurance agency has people on their team who take inbound calls from customers. That's the person you call when you want to add a car or make another change. The Richmond Agency used to be organized that way. But a few years ago, they divided that customer service group into two teams. The red team handles inbound calls. And there is a yellow team that makes outbound calls prior to your renewal. Those yellow team members are proactive. They'll frequently re-shop your coverage needs among different carriers without you even asking them to do that. Imagine getting a call from your insurance agent who said, "We were looking at your policy and found another insurance company that can give you the exact same coverage for 15 percent less." What would a call like that say to you? I know it would make me feel that I could trust this agency to be looking out for my best interests. That's going to make me a more loyal customer for sure. I'd think you were working for me!

Loyal customers create lower churn. That's a big deal. Lower churn means you start at a higher level of business each year. Since implementing the two-team approach, the Richmond Agency's churn has dropped significantly. That's huge for their bottom line, especially in a time where their competition with companies like Geico or Farmers, called direct writers in the insurance business, is more intense than ever. This is a time of significant pressure for independent insurance agents because of the competition. Many are struggling. But rather than lower expenses and hunker down, the Richmond Agency has increased outreach and is winning.

And just to put some icing on the cake, Brian told me that the yellow team actually finds new business as a result of their outbound calls. Many months, they write as much new volume as a producer working full time going after new customers would write. If you are keeping score, here's what the Richmond plan creates: less churn, increased loyalty, and lots of additional revenue. Makes you wonder why that approach is so rare.

It's Their Money

Most salespeople don't really understand how business math impacts decision-making for businesses. But when you start to believe you work for them, business math is very important to know.

Jim Stoos is one of the star consultants at Jim Doyle and Associates. He shared a story about how coming to understand the business reality of a client's business completely changed the dynamics of a conversation. The salesperson couldn't understand why the customer was hesitating on a decision that seemed incredibly logical. By probing further, they discovered what the real issue was. The amount of this commitment exceeded the company's entire net profit for the previous year. So while the decision seemed easy on the surface, it was actually very tough for this business owner. When the sellers connected with that reality, they were able to help the business owner find another way to fund the commitment and quickly closed the sale.

Understanding that it's their money is fundamental to the way Hearst's Rhonda Kuhlman approaches her clients.

According to Rhonda, "You work for the owner that you're dealing with and spend the money like it was coming out of your pocketbook." She was quick to add, "It's not like they have just this infinite amount of money to spend on advertising." Spend the money like it is your own. Spend the customer's money with a deep respect for the business issues that customers face. That often means taking time to get yourself educated about what profit/loss statements look like for their business.

The Richmond Agency's Brian Richmond lives that principle with his commercial insurance clients as well as the personal lines customer: "We love to save them dollars and be more efficient, but it's really to improve their business. It's bringing solutions to them. To me, I think our team should be an extension of their team. We're not on their payroll, but we're like that. That's what you should be doing."

You Actually Have Two Bosses

Our Servant Heart Sellers repeatedly told us they see themselves as working for their clients. But they also know they work for their company, as well. They have responsibility to serve both of their bosses. And many of the Servant Heart Sellers we interviewed for this book suggested that can occasionally be a little challenging.

Servant Heart Sellers will fight for their client's best interests inside their companies. But they also need to serve the best interests of their company. Does this create conflict? Occasionally, for sure. But the conflicts are almost always minimal, what Rhonda Kuhlman calls "a healthy professional disagreement." That can happen as managers and sellers work to figure out how to serve both parties' interests. It's almost always pretty benign. While it's rare, some great sellers have left companies that they feel don't reflect their values. It can be hard for a Servant Heart Seller to work for a company (or manager) that doesn't have some understanding of the passion for customer results these sellers feel.

The people we interviewed for this book and the hundreds of Servant Heart Sellers I've met in my career want to create great outcomes for their customers. But they almost always know they have a responsibility to the company that gives them their paycheck. Because these sellers are so good, they will push their bosses. They are sometimes not easy to manage. That's why, later in this book, there is a chapter for bosses on managing Servant Heart Sellers. But it's worth the occasional conflict to have these superstars working for your company and for their clients.

I Work for Them!

Servant Heart Sellers have such an intense drive to make a difference for their customers that they actually believe that their role is to act like they are employed by their customers. So when we talk about becoming an unpaid member of the customer's team, that's a position they work to achieve. For sure, there are some customers who might not be receptive to that. But that is always the goal for these sellers. And they believe it creates huge wins for them. Liberty Coach's Dave Wall was very clear about that. He says, "You're working for them, but they're also working for you. They're telling everybody about their experiences, why they have what they have, and who they purchased it from. It's all a bigger part of the puzzle."

The Servant Heart Sellers' Difference

The idea that "I work for them" wouldn't occur to most salespeople. It's the difference between a transactional relationship and one based on a desire to create partnerships with customers. It's not that salespeople don't care about their customers. Many do. So, what's the difference? It's a salesperson making a decision that is good for the customer even if that decision might have a negative short-term consequence for them. You might have been able to tell how impressed I was by the Richmond Agency's effort to look for better options for their customers. That will sometimes cost them commission. It takes more time. And it is completely different from the way most insurance agents work. Working that way requires a firm belief that in the end, if you take incredible care of your customers, you will win. I love that commitment.

PLAY THE LONG GAME

I THINK THE REASON THAT I AM LIKE THIS IS BECAUSE
I FEEL LIKE I'M IN THIS FOR THE LONG HAUL. I'VE BEEN
HERE FOR TWENTY-FIVE YEARS, AND I ALWAYS FEEL LIKE
IF I DO THE RIGHT THING BY THE CLIENT, THEY'RE GOING
TO BE THERE FOR A LONG TIME. I DON'T WANT TO SAY
ANYTHING THAT'S NOT TRUE. I DON'T WANT TO BURN ANY
BRIDGES. I WANT THEM TO BE CLIENTS FOR A LIFETIME,
NOT JUST CLIENTS FOR THIS WEEK OR NEXT WEEK.
—BARBARA ANDERSON

DO YOU HAVE A SALES QUOTA OR REVENUE BUDGET? Most
every salesperson I know does.

Make no mistake. Our Servant Heart Sellers are high achievers. They achieve their sales quotas and more. Most of the people interviewed for this book have won awards from their companies, often many, many times.

By the criteria that most salespeople are judged by, these folks are stars. And yet they would tell you that making budget or achieving their sales goals is the *result* of the work they do, not the *goal*. They are focused, not so much on making budget but on making a difference for their customers. And they know that the more they make a difference, the more likely they are to have high performance.

Short Term vs. Long Term

There is a huge difference between the transactional seller and the Servant Heart Seller. The transactional seller (aka, the peddler) is totally focused on making the sale. That's their biggest goal. They want to make a sale. The contrast? The Servant Heart Seller is focused on the account. This kind of seller thinks long term. Servant Heart Sellers have a strong belief that if it's good for the client, it will ultimately be good for them. That's easy to say but a lot harder to live, especially if what is good for the client has a significant negative impact on you and your commission. That's when the rubber meets the road.

This book is being written six months into the COVID-19 pandemic. Can you imagine how freaked out a business would be about spending money on advertising when the world was in shutdown mode in April and May 2020? That's what Rhonda Kuhlman was dealing with from her clients. You think businesses in your city were freaked out during this time? Try selling advertising in Orlando, where the big employers are companies like Disney, Universal, and SeaWorld. It was no surprise that

Kuhlman had a huge number of her clients calling to cancel their advertising in the first months of the COVID-19 pandemic. She said, "When all the shutdowns started happening, we took every cancellation, every pause in a campaign, and we took it with a smile on our face, and we said, 'Whatever you need from us, we'll do. You want to be off today, and you want to be back on at midnight the next night because you woke up and had a crazy idea? Call me. We'll figure it out.'"

Contrast that response to some of the competitors in Orlando. Some media outlets were trying to hold people to a two-week cancellation policy. That would mean an advertiser would be spending money (a scarce resource if you are essentially closed down) because the media outlet was more concerned about their needs than the customer's. That's short-term thinking. Good for the company but horrible for their customer.

Rhonda and her company made the right decision for their customers. They handled it that way even though it was not immediately good for them. You have to believe that most of those customers will remember that in the future. So that decision, as hard as it was, will ultimately be very good for Rhonda and her company. Short-term pain but long-term gain. That's what playing the long game is sometimes all about.

This can be a hard principle to live, especially if you are new in sales and need the commission. I understand that. In the earliest years of my sales training business, I only sold training days. I typically sold only eight days a month. So if a client wanted to cancel two days, that represented a 25 percent hit on my monthly income. In those days, a 25 percent hit felt like a major catastrophe. So to protect myself, I had strict contract language that kept things on the calendar. But things happen.

A client with a small sales staff had hired me for a two-day session. In the two weeks before the scheduled date, they lost one of their five sellers and had another leave for long-term disability. They called and wanted to cancel because they now were spending a lot of money to train just three people. My first reaction to that call? I can tell you it wasn't as customer friendly as Rhonda Kuhlman's! I was scared about the financial hit.

But as I was talking to the customer, I heard myself thinking about the message of my own seminars: "If it's good for the client, it will ultimately be good for you." At that moment, I will admit I hated hearing that voice! But I couldn't ignore the reality. Yes, I could force them to honor their contract, and they would have done that. But that would have not been good for them. So I (reluctantly) agreed we'd delay the session until they had a team back to full force. The right decision for them, for sure, but a painful short-term hit for me.

As it turns out, that decision was also the right one for our company, as well. We continued to work with that client for the next five years, generating tens of thousands in revenue for us. What would have happened if I had forced them to honor their contract and made them do my session as scheduled? I am positive I would have never worked with them again. "If it's good for the customer, it will ultimately be good for me." I had to believe that. And I had to live it!

Where Do You Invest Your Time?

A successful mortgage broker processes and closes five home loans per month. If you do that volume, that would put you in the top 5 percent of mortgage brokers around the country. How about Jeff Wagner? Jeff and his team actually do fifty to sixty loans per month—ten times the amount of a typical top performer. That is incredible.

Jeff gets 90 percent of his business as referrals from realtors and builders. I'm guessing that's typical of most mortgage brokers. But what's not typical is how much time Jeff invests in his referral network and how many referrals he gets because of that investment.

Jeff has a clear list of who gives him business. He meets with those people constantly. Jeff told me that after many years, those meetings are less about specific business issues and more a general catch-up with people who have become good friends. Jeff doesn't take this critical asset for granted—ever. He invests the time to stay in touch with them, week after week, month after month.

Although Jeff considers his referral sources his friends, it's not just about the relationship. Jeff knows his programs might not be a fit with all the home buyers who call him. But he will spend time to educate a buyer even if they end up working with someone else. Why? It's not just because he has a heart of service. He wants that prospect to tell their real estate broker that Jeff gave them advice that was truly helpful. If the realtor gets that feedback, it's likely that realtor will send more people to Jeff.

Jeff is playing a long game. He doesn't want a few referrals from you. He wants lots of referrals. And he wants them for a long time. So he invests the time to build relationships and keeps doing it.

RV super seller Dave Wall knows where most of his customers can be found. They are living in their big coaches, frequently in very fancy "campgrounds." He knows where to find them in the winter in Florida or during the summer in the mountains of North Carolina. He knows a bunch will be at the big motorcycle rally in Sturgis, South Dakota, each summer. So where is Dave? He's there with his coach, hosting parties and spending time with his customers—and coincidentally, meeting their friends, who may not *yet* be Dave's customer.

In our UPGRADE Selling seminars, I used to talk about Randy Watson so often that people started asking me if I paid him a royalty on his ideas. I learned so much from Randy. If you were a large customer of Randy, you were hearing from him all the time with what I call "nonselling" sales contacts. It might be an article from a business magazine he thought you would be interested in or a thank-you note. Commission salespeople who are essentially self-employed have to be very mindful of how they spend their time. Why would Randy spend time doing things like sending articles month after month when most salespeople never do that? He knew that it made a huge statement to the client that he gave a damn about them and their business. As the late Zig Ziglar used to say, "Nobody cares how much you know until they know how much you care."

Servant Heart Sellers invest their time in a way that reflects a long-term view. Are they afraid that time investment might occasionally be wasted? I suspect they seldom think about that. Sure, they know businesses get sold or go broke or leaders sometimes leave. Occasionally their effort doesn't have an immediate quid pro quo. But I am positive the sellers interviewed for this book would tell you that they *never* think about that. That's because they have seen so much value for thinking long term that they have no concerns about the times where it doesn't seem to have an immediate payout. They are playing the long game!

Don't Be Liked—Be Trusted

If you were to look up Servant Heart Selling in the dictionary, you might see a picture of David Melville. Our company was privileged to have David work for us for a long time. But before he was on our team, he worked for a client we served.

One day, I was making a call with David on a Chevrolet dealer. The dealer made a point of taking me aside to tell me his impression of David. He said, "When David first started calling on me, he said he wanted to be the best rep that had ever called on me. He asked me what he could do to become that. I told him ... get to know our business. So for the next twenty weeks, he took home one of the videos we used to train our people. Not only did he watch it, but he would come in and ask me questions about things he had watched."

I ask you, what kind of statement did David make to that dealer?

There's a belief by many that effective selling is about being likable. And that can't hurt for sure. But being liked isn't the goal. The goal is to be trusted because trust is the first step to becoming a true partner with your customer. When you start playing the long game—investing time that technically isn't just about making the next sale—the result is trust.

David's actions told his dealer that he was not just another seller. He cared. And that changed their relationship forever.

And I can't resist one final thought about David. He impressed his client. But that wasn't even the biggest win from that effort. David learned about the car business in a way that most salespeople would never do. So his time investment didn't just help him with *this* dealer; it helped him with call after call over the next years. That's playing the long game.

It's a Career, Not a Job!

Here's how I found the people whom I interviewed for this book. I asked friends and colleagues who would understand the book's direction for names of people they thought about when I used the term Servant Heart Selling. I knew only three of the people whom I reached out to. The others were referrals from friends and colleagues.

One of the things that genuinely surprised me was how many of these amazing sellers had been in the same jobs, often working with the same customers, for twenty to thirty years.

If you are relatively new to sales, you probably can't imagine working for the same company that long. I get that. I was like that early in my career.

I think this might be one of those "What came first? The chicken or the egg?" questions. Our group generally has had significant financial success. They love their work and their clients. Some of them told me that they had thought about moving into management at different points in their career but for one reason or another decided that it either wasn't the right time for them or didn't fit their skills. What was clear in our discussion is that they still have incredible enthusiasm for what they do. I think that's because the motivation for them is to have impact for their clients, not just to make a sale.

The question you might ask is this: should you reject the long game ideas if you are planning to move on from your current role in the next few years? I hope not. I can promise you that sellers with a Servant Heart have success that gets noticed. So you will get even bigger opportunities if that is your choice, opportunities both with your current employer or with another, and certainly more opportunities than you would ever have if you decided to keep being a transactional seller.

Can No Mean Not Yet?

My friend and former colleague John Hannon had a great response when a client would tell him no. He'd ask them, "Is that no for today or no for forever?" Sometimes they would tell him it was no for forever. And he'd move on. But more often their response would be that it wasn't a no forever, which meant he still would have an opportunity down the road.

AJ Vaden would agree. She told me, "I found, for me, that I was more than happy to play the long game. One of my core philosophies was that I never hear no. I just process that as not right now. Never no; it's just not right now. And that's just playing the long game."

AJ believes most salespeople lack patience. They don't have the patience or the endurance to do the things necessary to do it the right way. They're so pressured by the "I have to pay my bills. I have to get this sale." They don't have a patience to wait it out and play the long game. They're very short sighted.

The *Long, Long* Game

I've been a fan of Jim McIngvale for a long time. McIngvale, also known as Mattress Mac, is the owner of Houston-based Gallery Furniture. Gallery Furniture is widely recognized as one of the most successful firms in the furniture industry. One of their stores supposedly does more revenue per square foot than any furniture store in America. He's had mega success for a very long time.

Mac is a Servant Heart Seller for sure. And the stories of his service to Houston are legendary. When Hurricane Harvey dumped between fifty and seventy inches of rain on Houston, Mac opened two of his stores as shelters for people who were made homeless by the storm. As the storm was getting bad, he rented a fleet of trucks that could make it through the deep water to do rescues. But he didn't have any drivers. So he did a Facebook Live asking for people who could drive commercial rigs to come to his store and then sent those trucks out to do rescues and bring people back to his locations for a warm, dry place to stay.

I guess that lots of those folks bought furniture from Gallery over the next year!

When I caught up with Mac for this book, he shared his latest project. He has taken twenty-five thousand square feet of one of his stores and converted it to a free trade school. He's doing it in conjunction with Houston Community College and Work Texas. Students will go to school four days a week to learn a trade. They'll end up becoming either carpenters, mechanics, welders, or electricians. At the end, they go from laborer jobs to full-time careers in the trades. Mac isn't charging them for the schooling. They work one day a week for Gallery, and that's their tuition. Why would he do that? "We're going to be raising our own customers," he says. "We're going to be going to help them go out and get a good job, get a good income, and they'll be customers for life. So we do it because it's the right thing to do. But if you do right, I think it comes back to you."

Raising our own customers. That's playing the long, long game.

The Servant Heart Sellers' Difference

These first two lessons—I Work for Them and Playing the Long Game—are the attitudinal characteristics of Servant Heart Sellers. I think that's another way of saying they are foundational to the way they approach their business. Many, many salespeople would say they are that way, but it's seldom reflected in the way they work.

Short-term sellers want to make a sale. Long-term thinkers want to make a difference. Short-term sellers see the customer as an immediate opportunity. Long-term sellers are more focused on the lifetime value of a customer. And that will change the decisions they make.

Short-term thinkers often don't realize that the decisions they make about a customer today will impact the relationship they will have with their customers for a long, long time.

If the best interest of your customer is in conflict with your personal interests, what wins out? If you first swallow hard but then do what's right for your customer, you may be on your way to becoming a Servant Heart Seller.

❧ LESSON 3 ❧

ASK A MILLION QUESTIONS

WHENEVER YOU MEET SOMEBODY, IN THEIR OWN MIND,
THEY ARE ASKING YOU THREE QUESTIONS. NUMBER 1,
"DO YOU KNOW WHAT YOU'RE DOING?" NUMBER 2, "CAN
I TRUST YOU?" AND NUMBER 3 IS, "DO YOU CARE ABOUT
ME?" —DEAN THIBAULT

WHEN BILL GANGLOFF WAS A NEWBIE SALESPERSON, HE
CALLED ON A CAR DEALER. He was trying to "sell" this dealer.
But it turns out, the dealer gave him advice Bill has never forgotten.

Bill said that the dealer told him, "You're showing." And
when Bill quizzically asked what that meant, the dealer said,
"You are showing how much you want to sell me." And guess
what? That seldom works.

What does work? Servant Heart Sellers would tell you to

really try to understand what the customer needs, what they are trying to accomplish, before you start selling them.

One of my favorite lines is "Prescription without diagnosis is malpractice." Imagine this: you call up a doctor, and they want to give you a prescription before they have even heard your symptoms. If that happened to you, I'm guessing you would think that was not a great doctor. For physicians, that's likely malpractice. But for most salespeople, that's just the way they do it. And it's also malpractice. Take a guess at how many times each day the salespeople in your industry approach a customer with guns blazing. I will guarantee you it is likely in the 80 percent range. A very low percentage of salespeople really take the time to find out what the customer is really trying to accomplish before they launch into why they are the perfect solution for the customer.

In other words, they are showing. And showing will hurt your sales effectiveness, not help it.

When Dean Thibault talks about the sales process his commercial bankers use for Landmark National Bank, he focuses on the critical importance of the diagnosis step. Dean believes that humility is a key sales word and that being humble requires a seller (aka a commercial banker) to really understand a prospective customer's business issues before offering a solution.

The Landmark team uses an approach on a first meeting I find works in many industries. Dean calls it "the negative opening." It's a great technique to start a meeting with a new prospect.

Mr. or Ms. Prospect, we appreciate you taking the time to sit down with me today. I don't know if there's anything that we can do to help you with or not. You run a successful business. You have a great reputation, but if it's okay with you, I'll ask you a few questions . . . you can ask me a few questions. Within thirty minutes, we'll know whether there's anything there that we ought to follow up this meeting with another meeting, or if we decide to say thank you and part company.

A negative opening makes a couple of important statements to a client. It says that there won't be any pressure to buy anything today because the seller is just learning. And it says we are going to work together to see if there's something here that can make a difference for you and your situation. That approach quickly begins to establish the trust that is ultimately key to making a sale.

But it also takes the pressure off the salesperson. AJ Vaden sold very expensive coaching programs to big companies. Her first meetings were always diagnosis based. She says, "I just felt that the pressure completely went away in the consultative sales process because you knew upfront it's not happening on the first call."

What's the Customer Really Buying?

Why is diagnosis so important? It's because what you sell isn't really what the customer buys.

This is a critical insight. Dave Wall sells incredibly expensive motor coaches, the kind rock stars and rich entrepreneurs buy. A coach can cost as much as $2 million. But are customers really buying a coach? Or are they buying a lifestyle? That's why when Dean meets a new prospect, he'll focus on the "why." Why are they looking at this? What appeals to them? Have they sold a business or decided to sell a boat? What's the triggering event that brings them to considering this purchase? In that way, he gets an understanding of what their real motivation is.

There's an old line that captures what I mean. Five thousand times a week, customers go into hardware stores to buy a quarter-inch drill bit. But no one wants a quarter-inch drill bit. They want a quarter-inch hole!

Here's what that means: I spent my entire career in the advertising business and called on thousands of businesses. I can assure you, I got a lot more effective when I realized that my customers and prospects did not want to spend a single dollar on advertising. Not one dollar! They didn't want advertising. What they wanted was the things that advertising could do for them: grow their business, deal with a competitive threat, promote a new location or new service, or help them promote a going out of business sale. Advertising was just vehicle to accomplish those things. But they didn't want to spend any money on advertising. So it was essential to find out what they really wanted to accomplish. That's the hole. The advertising solution is the drill bit. Truly customer-focused sellers sell holes and not drill bits. And that requires being a question asker.

Brian Richmond sells personal lines insurance in a third-generation family agency in Wisconsin. He knows his customers don't want to spend a dime on insurance. They want security for their home or family. They want to manage risk for their company or provide their employees better, affordable healthcare. When Brian first meets clients, he doesn't have a clue what they really want. His approach to an initial meeting? Here's how he describes it: "My goal is to uncover what their needs are and figure out if it matches the skill set of what I have and if I can bring something of value. I've had people say before, 'Oh, you sell insurance?' I say, 'No, I don't sell anything. I provide coverage that people want.'"

Think about what you sell. And then go deeper. Think about what the customer is really buying—the hole and not the drill bit. The purpose of questioning is to really get clear on what each customer's "hole" looks like. Without a doubt, this is the most critical step to real sales success.

Don't Be the Peddler

In olden days, the peddler rode their wagon from town to town selling stuff. Today's peddler doesn't have a wagon or horse. They travel with a fancy leather folio or a backpack. But they are peddling just the same. It's the way a huge percentage of sellers operate.

"Here's what I've got."

"This would be great for you."

Isn't that sad? When I wrote the paragraph above, I initially thought it was sad. But then I realized that Servant Heart Sellers might say that the fact that most salespeople are peddlers is actually great for them. Really great! It's a lot easy to differentiate yourself when your competitors are mediocre. What's the line about "in the land of the blind, the one-eyed man is king?"

This is important. If you connect with this idea, it will forever change how you sell. Too many salespeople are going into a client with guns blazing. Here's what I've got. Peddlers are pitching things. They spend almost no time in diagnosis. Or they'll handle a call with what I call "fake" diagnosis, asking the minimum amount of questions possible, and then saying something that sends this statement: "Well, enough about you ... let's talk about me."

Servant Heart Sellers couldn't be more different. They ask lots and lots and lots of questions, questions that help determine the real issues driving a client's decision-making.

One way you can tell how close you are to becoming a Servant Heart Seller is to look at how much time you spend in the diagnosis part of the sales process. Well-known trainer Don Beveridge would say that customer-focused salespeople spend two to three times longer asking questions than the peddler does. And Servant Heart Sellers are even more committed to diagnosis time than that. There's a simple reason for all the questions they ask. Their real commitment is to delivering impact for their customers. And they can't honor that commitment and make a difference to their clients if they don't have any understanding of what that customer's challenges, issues, and opportunities are all about.

The Power of Preparation and System

Lots of Servant Heart Sellers are like Hearst's Barbara Anderson. They are naturally inquisitive. They have an innate curiosity about how a client's business works. The diagnosis step is very natural and comfortable for them. But for others, it isn't as easy. They can't wing it. They have to be prepared to ask better questions.

I've been teaching diagnosis for a long time in sales training seminars—thirty years at least. But here's what's funny: so many of the questions I taught media sales executives to ask can now be answered way before you ever meet the customer. Today, we can learn much about a client by simply checking them out online. It's important to not waste a customer's time with questions when the answer can be easily found. That way, you can use your time to ask about more significant issues.

Suppose you are calling on a new business prospect for a bank or an insurance agency. How can you get a better understanding of that business before you even walk in the door? At the very minimum, you should check out their website, look at their Facebook business page, review your prospect's LinkedIn profile, and have a sense of the business issues they face.

There's a big reason why the preparation is so significant. It's the difference between just asking questions ("How's business?" "How long have you owned the company?") and asking the kinds of questions that really get into the real issues the prospective client is facing—the "find the hole" questions.

Doing my homework changes everything. I'm able to say things like, "I looked at your website and noticed X. How is that impacting your business?" That question leads to a business conversation rather than just asking a few mostly superficial questions.

The Common Diagnosis Call Mistakes

It's been my experience that salespeople make three mistakes in diagnosis.

Mistake 1: They think they are doing diagnosis simply

because they are asking questions. But if their questions are just a few blah-blah generic questions, that's not close to enough. They need to be asking the kind of questions that really determine the customer's needs. The best questions get to the real issues or motivation for that customer.

Mistake 2: Jim Stoos is a senior consultant for our company. He is clearly a Servant Heart Seller. He makes sales calls side by side hundreds of sellers each year. Stoos believes that one of the big mistakes sellers make is what he calls "self-referencing." He says, "Many sellers want to tell the client what they should be doing based upon their own experiences. That's called self-referencing. And self-referencing is the worst thing we can do because we don't really know." Stoos says, "There's nothing wrong with drawing from your own experience, but when you self-reference and then try to base your purchasing habits and translate that to someone else, you need to learn more. Don't put your foot in your mouth."

I think Jim Stoos is on to something big. Effective sellers leave their egos—and their preconceived ideas—at the door. Even when they *think* they know the answer, they keep their opinions and ideas to themselves during the diagnosis process. Actually, it is more than just keeping your mouth shut. It's truly keeping your brain quiet and really listening to what the customer is saying. Great salespeople listen fully to a customer's answer. They don't have their next question in mind. They frequently ask a follow-up question: "What is that important?"

Mistake 3: A seller starts the diagnosis process correctly. They start asking questions. But the minute the client says something that they think gives them an opportunity, they pounce and immediately turn from questioner to seller. Doing this will hurt you and reduce your effectiveness. You'll absolutely be seen as a peddler by that client. That alone is bad. But it's also extremely likely there was a bigger issue that customer needs to deal with that you never learned about. And you'll never discover that because you switched too quickly to sales mode.

Having a selling process that you get comfortable with and then use on every call is huge. Many salespeople use at minimum a two-call process. A diagnosis call, or two, gets followed by a meeting where the seller brings a possible solution. But Al Fox, who runs a big investment practice, says it can be more: "For you, it might be three meetings; for someone else, it might be five. But generally as a seasoned professional, if I can get your data and understand your goals, I'll have a good idea of your needs in about an hour."

Al Fox is so focused on the customer he doesn't even have a predetermined idea of how long the questioning and information gathering part of the process should take. It takes what it takes for him to feel comfortable that he might have a solution that makes sense.

AJ Vaden shared about almost having a clock in her head to limit her diagnosis calls to about an hour. As she kept refining her approach, AJ created a pre-call questionnaire with an upward of twenty questions. And she wouldn't even schedule the first diagnosis meeting until she had the questionnaire back. When she started using that approach, she found her diagnosis meetings led to even deeper conversations. AJ would never have a "how's business" diagnosis meeting. She's talking about real issues and therefore getting real clarity about if or how she can help. That gives her incredible confidence to go back in her subsequent meeting, knowing she has a solution that has a track record of solving her clients' challenges.

Lather, Rinse, Repeat

One day, I asked a seller why he thought a team member was so effective. He said, "She's like the back of the shampoo bottle." Seeing my confusion, he continued, "You know. Where it says lather, rinse, and repeat."

Talk to a Servant Heart Seller and you'll find out that they have a process they use repeatedly. They start by doing very effective diagnosis calls with lots and lots of great questions. These are deeper discussions because they have taken the time to prepare. Shamire Goodwin told me, "Usually, I'm pretty educated. I never go into a new business call without preparing. With the amount of information that is available to us, a seller should have their act together when they get to that face-to-face time. It eliminates all the extraneous time spent on asking them questions that will sometimes annoy them."

Shamire believes that customer will open up because you're asking them about things that are important to them. But the questioning process also makes a statement that you've done your homework. As Shamire says, "Typically, people open right up, and the conversation blossoms from there."

Servant Heart Sellers follow diagnosis by bringing the customer ideas to deal with the issues that are discussed. They follow that process consistently. Again and again and again!

Acute Listening

★ **YOU** ★
MUST BE
PRESENT
TO WIN

I have tremendous respect for Rory Vaden. He is considered one of the best professional speakers on the planet. That is literally the truth. Years ago, Rory was twice a finalist for Toastmasters World Championship. Today, he speaks to some of the most prestigious audiences and conferences around the world.

Rory is a speaker. Speakers talk! It's what we do. But Rory thinks that one of the most significant attributes of a Servant Heart Selling is what he calls acute listening. That's way beyond just listening.

Rory describes it like this: "It's being interested. It's not just hearing. Hearing is I'm not talking. Listening is I am taking the words that you are actually saying and taking them in. But, to me, acute listening is that as you talk, I'm trying to decipher whether or not what I have is something that can help you get where you really want to go. And if what I have is something that can help you get to where you really want to go, how can I connect the dots for you?"

Rory describes acute listening like being able to hear a pin drop in a crowded room. Most salespeople are good talkers. But Servant Heart Sellers work hard to be better listeners. In fact, some of the folks we interviewed for this book specifically talked about wanting to continue to improve in that area. That's my story as well. Stephen Covey wrote the bestselling book, *The 7 Habits of Highly Effective People*. In that book his line about listening to understand really speaks to me. I have had lots of time when I didn't practice acute listening. And I am sure that some of the people I work (and live with) today likely think I still do that. For many years, a lot of the selling I did was on a tight schedule. I had appointments set for me every ninety minutes. Being late was not cool. One day, I had a realization about how self-centered I could be. I realized that I never checked my watch to see if we were running late when I was talking. I only did that when the customer was speaking. Was I really listening? I don't think so.

A really common mistake salespeople make is listening just to reply, thinking of the next question before they ever completely hear the customer's answer or—more dangerously—not even asking another question as they respond to what the client has said and start selling.

I love the "Must Be Present to Win" slogan. Whether it's with my wife or kids, on the golf course, or in front of a customer, if I am truly present, I am able to be better. A better husband. A better dad. A better friend. And definitely a better listener. And that makes me a lot more effective salesperson.

Rory Vaden says his wife and business partner AJ is by far the best salesperson in their family and one of the best sellers he's ever seen. AJ believes that one of the most important attributes of successful salespeople is the desire to learn, and that can only be accomplished by a practicing acute listening. AJ has trained lots of salespeople as part of her work. And she believes, sadly, that great listening skills are rare among salespeople.

We teach salespeople lots of things to say. But we don't spend nearly enough time talking about the critical importance of listening. And that is an improvement opportunity for many of us. Even some of the people interviewed for this book admit to working to become better listeners. It's something I work on as well. I love Rory Vaden's acute listening. I think that means really being present. I can feel it when I am doing that. I aspire to do it more consistently. It can and will make a huge difference.

The Probing Never Stops

Some of the folks reading this may sell something that is a one-time sale. But most sellers want to work with customers for a long time. That means your questioning never stops. It's something to keep doing and doing and doing—always striving to go deeper in understanding a client's business or challenges.

Barbara Anderson talks about having clients she's known for over twenty years. And she's still asking questions to learn more about their business. That's a Servant Heart Sellers' concept. And it works because no customer stays the same. The issues that drove a customer's need for a bank loan or for an advertising program are always changing. Last year's solution may not be the right solution today. A business may have needed a bank initially to fund an acquisition or expansion. But ten years later, the owner is exploring ways to sell to the management team. Servant Heart Sellers recognize that change is a constant. So they never stop asking questions.

When I was building the UPGRADE Selling System, the selling process we teach our clients, I wanted to make sure that sellers understood that diagnosis wasn't "one and done." So we named our diagnosis call a "time-out call." Yes, it's an approach used for first meetings with new prospects. But it's even more powerful as a time-out in an existing game. You say something like "Before we talk about next year or next quarter, I'd like to take a time-out and make sure I am completely up to speed on all the issues you are facing." Time-outs pause the basketball game so the teams can regroup and see where they are. It's the same concept for Servant Heart Sellers.

The questions never stop because the desire to serve never stops.

A Final Thought for Those New to Sales

My friend and mentor Frank Wheeler has a way of asking me probing questions that usually take a long time to answer. But this day, I responded quickly. He asked me what I thought was the biggest reason I had been successful. I immediately answered, "I've asked a million questions."

It's true. I love to find out about what people do and what their business issues are. I am constantly asking questions. I am also naturally inquisitive.

An aside—a few weeks after I gave Frank my answer, I actually calculated that in a fifty-year sales career, a million questions work out to about four hundred questions per week.

I've probably missed that number by a few weeks, but I have to be pretty close to the million question mark. I am sure that when my kids were teenagers, they thought I asked them a million questions each some days!

If I had a magic wand and could impart one piece of advice to new salespeople, it would be to focus on asking questions— well-prepared, business-oriented questions. If you become a nonstop questioner, that single skill will have so much impact on your career and your success.

Want a successful career in sales? Ask a million questions.

The Servant Heart Sellers' Difference

Let me be blunt: I have spent thousands of hours with sales-people. And 90 percent don't spend nearly enough time on the diagnosis step of the sales process. They seldom ask enough questions. Or, as discussed above, they ask questions without hearing the answers, asking questions because they have been taught to do that without connecting the dots to how the answers might lead to understanding the customer's needs.

As a business owner, I get to see hundreds of pitches. In recent years, many of them come from messages on LinkedIn. The percentage of time that those messages have absolutely no idea what our company does is frightening. "This would be perfect for you"—and I am thinking as I read that, *Just leave me alone.* Peddlers for sure.

When I spend time with people who are new to sales, I usually tell them that if they want to be successful, they need to get really, really good at asking questions. Asking good questions is the fundamental difference between Servant Heart Sellers and the vast majority of salespeople. It is a difference maker. Maybe the biggest difference maker of all.

TEACH, DON'T SELL

THERE IS A SATISFACTION YOU GET WHEN YOU SHOW
SOMEBODY SOMETHING AND THEY'RE LIKE, THIS IS
GREAT. IT MAKES YOU FEEL BETTER AS A PERSON. I DON'T
THINK ANYBODY EVER SAYS TO A SALESPERSON, "THANK
YOU FOR SELLING ME THAT REALLY EXPENSIVE THING."
—PIERRE BOUVARD

ARBITRON PROVIDED RATINGS TO RADIO STATIONS FOR
DECADES BEFORE BEING SOLD TO NIELSEN IN 2013.

I hated Arbitron. Most people who owned or ran radio stations like I did hated Arbitron. Well, maybe the people who had good ratings liked them! But I owned what was about the number 14 ranked station in a ten-station market. So I hated them.

I hated the company. But I loved my Arbitron rep. And

nearly thirty years later, we are still friends.

Pierre Bouvard worked for Arbitron for a long time. He started as a trainer and had moved into sales when I met him. Many years later, he became President of Sales and Marketing for the company. Of all the salespeople who have ever personally called on me, Pierre probably most lived the principles of Servant Heart Selling.

His approach to sales, which later became the entire focus of the Arbitron sales process, was based on his beginnings as a trainer with the company.

At Arbitron, the trainer shows clients how to use the products they would buy. How can you manipulate the ratings data to create a sales story for this station? What's the best way to position this station versus its competitors? So trainers were focused from their earliest days with the company on how to make the Arbitron products work best for the client.

Bouvard shares, "We found that the best salespeople were the best trainers because they were really good at taking the station and saying, 'Hey, where can I find the sales stories? How can I best position this station?'"

The most effective Arbitron sellers realized that they should never stop doing the first job they were in. Bouvard says, "Even though you were now an account executive, the smartest thing you could do when you sat with your station is to act like you were their trainer. What objections are you getting? How are people criticizing your station? Well, let's try to figure out a way around that."

The sellers with a training background didn't come and immediately pitch you on a new Arbitron product. They came and showed you how the data would make your station look good. Pierre said his sellers learned this technique from a great trainer named Steve Marx. Marx suggested sellers used what he called "*how* selling, not *why* selling." Don't share all the reasons *why* a prospect should buy the product. Focus on *how* the product can help them. When you do that, your meeting and any presentation you bring will be a whole lot different—and a whole lot more effective.

Pierre used this approach with me several times while I was his client. For almost all that time, we were being incredibly careful about expenses. I didn't want to spend any more money, especially with Arbitron. But Pierre would bring a new product to me and show me how to use it in a way that made us look good. And usually I'd end up thinking, "We have to have this." And then I'd find the money somewhere.

You are probably asking if this approach created more results. After all, increasing results is the ultimate goal of any sales book you read. For Arbitron, the results were significant. Bouvard shares this:

> The effectiveness of those people who were primarily teachers was dramatically more. Because the people who were teachers would go into a new product, find that amazing sales story, create the one sheet, and actually give it to the station, and say, "Hey, I know you don't subscribe to us, but here you go." It was a like a free sample. "Would this be useful?" And usually the sellers are like, "This is awesome. Can I use this?" Sure, go ahead. How selling, not why selling! Teach them how to use that product. Giving them some free samples. There was no question that the people that were

training-based just did so much better. Station people took their calls. They wanted to talk to them.

Let's back up for just a second. To do that kind of selling, you must know the client's issues so that your entire presentation is focused on what they want to accomplish. This kind of presentation is based on a foundation of questioning and acute listening we outlined in the previous chapter: "Prescription without diagnosis is malpractice."

Jasmine Ruschmann is the Midwest Regional Sales Manager for RXBAR. She calls on grocery chains and convenience stores. When Jasmine gets a new buyer, she often offers them an Insights Presentation early in the relationship. She will tell them, "You're new to buying for this category. Would you be interested in doing an educational session with our insights team, and they can educate you on the category?" Jasmine positions it as teaching, not selling. "This is not just what's going on at RXBAR; it's like this is what's going on in the whole energy bar category." And sometimes that teaching, not selling approach gets the buyer's boss to join that presentation. That's because it's not about RXBAR—it's about the category. And anytime you can get more senior people in a meeting, that's good.

For independent insurance agent Brian Richmond, it's really thinking like you own the client's business. And then teaching them what insurance concerns they may have. Brian will say to a prospect, "You don't know me that well, but I'm just pretending that I own your company. I'm telling you that if I owned your company with my insurance background, this is how I would insure it."

Al Fox is a financial adviser with a big practice in Greater

Philadelphia market. He actually sees his entire approach to getting new clients as a teaching opportunity: "We look at ourselves as educators. When we do a really good job of educating, people follow a natural process that's at their pace. It allows them to absorb, understand, repeat back to us, and think about what they're doing, not make rushed decisions. They really take it in. That process is standard. The amount of time varies by the individual, based on them."

Fox says he'll say to clients, "At any point during this process, if you don't think it's going in the right direction or we don't think it's going in the right direction, please know that each of us has permission to stop, evaluate if we are on track, and decide if this is something we both should engage in moving forward."

He wants the prospective client to know that by the time they are done, "It'll be crystal clear whether or not we're the right fit and whether or not you want to engage us. If you're not the right fit, that's okay. We promise you, you'll be better educated as a result, and you'll make an even better decision for what you want, specifically."

I love what Al Fox told me: "You forget that not everyone is meant to be your client, not everyone is meant to receive your help, and not everyone sees what you provide as a solution for them." Amen!

As I've mentioned, I've spent my career selling (and helping others) sell advertising. Teach, don't sell is a cornerstone to our approach. In fact, we use a presentation model that starts with teaching.

Here's how our model works. It starts by outlining three ingredients that we believe are needed for an effective advertising program. During this part of the presentation, there is absolutely no discussion of any specific media or the station we are representing. It is simply an educational session on how advertising works. That's important. No selling here about a specific product, just an overview of what needs to be part of a high-impact advertising campaign. Our consultants and our TV station clients will make thousands and thousands of sales presentations each year. And there's almost never any disagreement from a customer about the first section of the presentations we do. This is the education part of a selling presentation.

Once the prospect has seen the ingredients they'll need to be successful, the rest of our time is to be specific about how the proposed plan deals with each of the three ingredients. We teach the three ingredients then fill in the details about each. This is *how* selling, not *why* selling.

Think about the really effective salespeople you have worked with. Even better, think about those who have sold you. I'm guessing that when you analyze their approach, you'll find they spend a lot of their time teaching. Whether it's the contractor who helps you see how a minor tweak can make the project a lot less expensive or the RV salesperson who shows you the difference between one towing option or another, effective salespeople are usually great teachers.

Paul McCauley is the financial adviser for my wife, Paula, and me. He's Managing Director of Merrill Lynch's McCauley-McGuirk Group in Boston. He is a big-time teacher. I am guessing he spends 45 percent of the time we are with us asking questions to determine what's changed since the last time we spoke. And he spends another 45 percent teaching us about how a specific investment fits in to our overall plan. And only about 10 percent of the time is he actually presenting us with something he thinks we should buy, and even that time has a teaching element to it. In his heart, Paul, like so many Servant Heart Sellers, is a teacher.

The Power of Enthusiasm

Salespeople who are enthusiastic about what they sell and enthusiastic about how their product can help a client are more effective.

But enthusiasm is a hugely misunderstood word. It's the not positive thinking "rah rah" that so many motivational speakers talk about: "I'm great! I can't pay my bill this week, but I'm GREAT!" You can say that with as much enthusiasm as you want . . . but you are still broke.

This is significant. Google the words "power of enthusiasm," and there are a lot of articles about how motivational speakers define enthusiasm. Don't misunderstand. I love motivational speeches as much as anyone. But telling someone to "fake it till you make it" is the absolute opposite of what Servant Heart Sellers believe.

My favorite definition of enthusiasm is remembering that the last four letters—*I A S M*—stand for I Am Sold Myself.

Servant Heart Sellers won't ever sell somebody something they don't believe in. There's no "fake it till you make it" about this. They must believe their solution is absolutely right for the client. Not sorta right—absolutely right. In fact, several of the sellers interviewed for this book told me about times when they had pushed back with their managers about something that was a company priority that they weren't yet convinced was in the best interest of this customer.

It is in the DNA of a Servant Heart Seller to have to believe that something is the absolute right choice for a customer. There's no middle ground for that. But when they feel their solution is right for the customer, then you'll see their approach be the real example of enthusiasm. I am sold myself.

The Servant Heart Sellers' Difference

Pull out your most recent presentation to a new customer. Look at every single page starting with the title. How many of those pages make a connection to how your product or service can help the customer? How many pages are all about you? I recently reviewed some presentations for a big company. These folks do great work and have some very prestigious clients. They offer real value to their customers. But their presentations were weak. They outlined the work they do, not how work that would most benefit the customer. Even their title page was about them. In fact, the whole presentation was about them. Impressive graphics, interesting use of technology, but their approach was really well-dressed peddlers with above-average PowerPoints. Such a missed opportunity to be more effective.

They were selling. And here is what I think: they really had no choice. They had to do it that way. That's because, I am willing to bet, their sellers were pretty weak at the diagnosis step. When that part of the process is weak, it's impossible to understand the customer's issues. That makes teaching instead of selling almost impossible.

CLOSING HARD—A QUICK PATH TO FAILURE

It's the biggest meeting space in Boston. This day, there are three thousand salespeople from all kinds of different industries waiting to be inspired and taught. I had brought my entire sales team down from Maine.

One of the keynote speakers was a leading sales guru of that time. His subject? Closing. It's often a common part of most sales trainers' seminars. This speaker came from the life insurance business. And he shared his absolute favorite closing technique to sell insurance: "If I am talking to some young parents and they have a couple of cute kids bouncing around, I'll tell them a story. I'll tell them how I had failed to sell a couple just like them with a couple of cute kids just like theirs. Unfortunately, I didn't make that sale. And how did I feel when a couple of months later, those parents were in a tragic accident that left those children orphans? 'If those parents were here today, what do you think they would tell you to do?'"

He told us this was his "back the hearse up to the door and let them smell the carnations" close. And I confess, as someone relatively new in my career, I was thinking, *I wonder how I could do that selling advertising?*

When you Google the term "closing the sale," you'll get 530 million responses. That should tell you how the idea of closing the sale permeates so many of the conversations about selling. Virtually every sales training program you will ever attend spends significant time talking about closing.

Most of them miss a real understanding about how commitment really occurs. Here's an example: I clicked one article on page I of the Google search. The article outlined a number of closing techniques a salesperson might try. One of their suggestions outlined a closing technique based on scaring the customer. Just like backing the hearse up to the door.

These are the exact words they suggested:

"I'd hate to see (some negative consequence) befall your company because you didn't have the right product in place. Do you want to take the crucial step to protect your organization today?"

I am sure some people reading that may say, "Wow, that's a great way to close." But I guarantee you that if you tried that on me, I might get sick—right before I asked you to leave.

The list of aggressive closing techniques that are being taught goes on and on and on. I read many of them and actually got mad.

"If we throw in [freebie], would that convince you to sign

the contract today?"

"Will you commit to doing business with us today?"

Those kinds of techniques make me gag. And I am convinced they don't work. You might disagree. But before you toss this book down and storm away, I need to be clear. There's a place in effective selling for asking for the order. It's important. But Servant Heart Sellers realize that being an aggressive closer absolutely doesn't work. In fact, aggressive closing can actually hurt your sales effectiveness more than it helps it.

When Neil Rackham was writing the legendary sales book, *SPIN Selling*, his team studied thirty-five thousand sales presentations. Their goal was to determine if learning how to be an aggressive closer would help sales effectiveness. What they discovered was significant.

If the price of the item was small and the transaction time brief, aggressive closing techniques would actually help you. You can see that every time you go through the drive-through at a fast-food restaurant: "Do you want to make that a combo?" When the person at the window asks you that question, that's a closing technique. I doubt that bothers anyone. After all, the time I am at that window is minimal (brief transaction time) and the price of a combo is low, so no one is offended. And guess what? Rackham's research showed those techniques increased sales effectiveness. More combos were sold, thus increasing revenue. I can only imagine how much money McDonald's made by getting their people to always ask "Do you want fries with that?" I am guessing it was *huge*.

But most sales are the opposite of the drive-through window. They are discussions that have taken more time. The products they sell are way more expensive than a Big Mac. They involve longer conversations about more money! When you use aggressive closing techniques in those situations, Rackham says you'll see your closing percentage actually go down.

Here's what is important to understand. The ideas of aggressive closing that are at the foundation of most sales training can *hurt* your effectiveness. When you close hard, you'll close less!

Rory Vaden was adamant about the danger in aggressive closing.

> I am not only unimpressed by the hard-closing tactics. I'm disgusted by them. I think this idea that sales is a battle between two people and that there will be a winner and a loser and that the client is the loser somehow, to me, is inhumane. It's disgusting. It's terrible. So the idea of touting how good I am at talking people into things they don't want or how successful I am at pressuring people to acquiesce after so many attempts is not something I'm interested in or that ever want our company's reputation to be associated with.

Look at the words Rory used: "disgusting," "terrible," and "incredibly ineffective."

Every Servant Heart Seller interviewed for this book talked about the need to secure commitment. But they universally would tell you that it's the by-product of doing the right things the right way. They are more focused on that than any specific closing technique.

Mike VanDevere is president of VanDevere dealerships in Akron, Ohio. You would expect a car dealership to be a place where aggressive closing was the norm. But not at the VanDevere's stores.

"We don't talk a lot about closing," he says. "We talk about how to do a better job for our customers. Customer retention is one of our big topics. If I've got good customer retention, then I would say I'm doing the right things. We're going about business in the right way. If we're focused on closing, we're treating the customer as a one-time opportunity and we're not big-picture oriented. We're focused on the long term."

VanDevere went on to say, "My real success comes from customer retention. How many customers do I get coming back to me and saying, 'I wouldn't go anyplace else. This is where I want to come because I'm treated like family, like a friend'? To me, that's what makes us different. To me, I know, and I share this with my people, customers can buy cars and get service anywhere. What makes us different—it's you, it's how you treat the customers. It's us, how we communicate. We treat them like friends and family."

A consistent message from Servant Heart Sellers is that when you are 1) committed to bringing great solutions to your customers and 2) spending a lot of time asking questions to really determine the customer's needs, then getting commitment gets easier.

For Hearst's Barbara Anderson, that focus on the process doesn't ever feel like a hard close. She says, "I feel like I really don't sell to them. I feel like I have conversations. And those conversations are really about . . . this is what I think I have. This is how it could work for you."

What Does Work?

Some of the people interviewed for this book would describe themselves as weak closers. I am in that group. I don't think I've ever been a hard closer. Don't misunderstand what I am saying. Even after fifty years in sales, I still get excited when a client says yes. Really excited. I can fist bump and high-five with the best. I love to close sales.

But even with that desire to make a sale, I never felt I was a great closer. And yet I have closed millions and millions of dollars of business. I do it by outlining exactly how our products can work to help the client either solve a problem they currently have or take advantage of an opportunity to grow their business.

The commonly used term for that way to get a commitment is assumptive closing. And it's my observation that most of the really great Servant Heart Sellers I see use this as their default way to get commitment.

In its simplest form, here's the process: first, spend way more time than most determining what their customer really needs or wants. Then bring back a well-thought-out plan to accomplish those goals.

After the seller has presented that plan, their "ask" for commitment often sounds like this:

"Ms. or Mr. Customer, we talked about how important it is for you to accomplish X. We've brought back a plan that does that and shares how similar efforts have helped our customers like you. Assuming that everything we've talked about makes sense, here's what we have to do from here to get this implemented."

It's simple. It's not manipulative in any way. But it does ask for commitment.

Think about the term "assumptive closing." As a seller, I am confident that I have done my homework. I feel incredibly confident that my solution will be good for my customer. So I move the process along, saying, "If this makes sense, here's where we need to go from here."

For Shamire Goodwin, it's that simple: "I simply ask people, 'I've identified all your challenges. I've met all those challenges with a strategy that you've agreed on. Can we move forward?' I ask for the sale because I've done everything they've asked me to do."

Don't Overthink It!

If you are new to sales, you could spend hours reading about all the possible closing techniques you could use. I'd encourage you to not waste your time doing that. So many of those techniques act like the purpose of selling is "I win and you lose," almost like you can somehow trick your client into buying. I guarantee you that those techniques will hurt you.

You don't need to overthink closing. Sometimes it's as simple as saying, "What do you think?" Use that simple technique after every presentation, and you will increase your effectiveness. You've asked for feedback, and when it is positive, you will know the client is ready to go forward.

Does This Make Sense?

One of my favorite lines to use when I am presenting to a client is "Does this make sense?" Some of the sales books might call this trial closing. But for me, it's simply pausing several times during my formal presentation and checking in with the customer: "Does what we just talked about make sense to you?"

If I do that a few times during my presentation, I can move to commitment with high confidence that we will be moving forward.

And what do I do when they say, "No, it doesn't make sense"? I go right back to asking questions. I need to quickly determine if it doesn't make sense because I haven't explained it well enough *or* it doesn't make sense because the customer disagrees. It is way better to know that in the middle of your presentation than to get a *no*, you don't really understand at the end. Asking "Does this make sense?" or "Do you connect to that idea?" or similar types of questioning several times during your presentation helps you see if what you have outlined is a solution your customer can agree with. Hearing positive answers to those questions makes "closing" much easier. Does that make sense to you?

Reduce Risk and Sell More

Here's a line I use all the time in my sales training sessions: "Selling is the process of taking away the buyer's risk."

I almost always immediately go on to say, "If there was no risk, the client would do it, right?" But there is always risk in the customer's mind that your solution won't work. That's because they haven't done it before. So the job of the salesperson is to make the leap of faith as small as possible for the customer.

In the past few years, I've gone even deeper with this idea of taking away risk. What if one of the principle goals of your sales presentation was to take away risk? How would you change your presentation to do that? What things would you be talking about?

There are lots of ways to take away risk. Think about the statement "money back guarantees" made to you when you are buying something. A guarantee takes away the risk of making a bad decision. And while most sellers can't make a guarantee like that, there are other ways to minimize the customer's risk, depending on the product that you sell.

Maybe it's a Return on Investment (ROI) analysis. That's how a friend who sells solar systems makes the decision less risky. He'll get copies of a prospect's electric bill and show them how quickly their initial investment is repaid. If you know that a combination of the tax credit and the electric bill reduction your system has paid for itself in fifty months, that makes the decision less risky.

My favorite way to reduce risk is by the use of case histories or success stories. There are some industries, like investments, where using case histories has regulatory issues. But for many sellers, sharing the positive experience of previous clients can help a prospective customer feel like this is a less risky decision.

Think about it this way: suppose this book was selling for $500, not $25. That would make the decision to buy it a lot more risky. A nice lunch costs $25. But $500 is a bigger deal. More risk, for sure. But suppose you found out that the last hundred people who had read this book had already seen their sales go up by 20 percent. Wouldn't that make the decision to spend $500 seem less risky? There's still risk. But the use of success stories makes that risk go down. Share stories and win sales.

Facts Tell, but Stories Sell

A huge percentage of people rely on data and facts to make decisions. So just telling stories is not going to be enough to close a sale. But when you present data and charts, make sure you also share a story (or, better yet, multiple stories) about the impact another customer has enjoyed because of your services or product.

I've long believed that if you want to learn a lot about sales, you might study those thirty-minute infomercials on TV. Think about the millions and millions of dollars in products sold by those messages. There's great training for salespeople in watching those. And it's cheap training for you—as long as you don't end up buying the no-fat fryer or the Total Gym workout program! There is one key ingredient in every single one of those programs. They all have lots and lots of customer testimonials.

I recently consulted with a company that brings digital marketing solutions to businesses all over America. When I reviewed their sales presentations and marketing materials, they were all about the technical solutions they could bring. These are smart people who do a great job for their clients. But I can guarantee them (and you) that they'll see their sales go up and increase their closing percentage if they add a bunch of client case studies and testimonials to their presentations and their materials.

Facts tell, but stories sell. The more client success stories you include in a presentation, the more impact you'll have. Why? Because every successful customer you (or your company) have successfully worked with minimizes the risk for a new client trying to make a decision—but only if you share those stories with the customer.

The Servant Heart Sellers' Difference

I hate aggressive closing. And I believe it hurts a salesperson's performance more than it helps it! And that's especially true if you are selling a more expensive product that requires multiple sales calls.

I hate training that still teaches what I think are manipulative closing tactics: "Oh, is your pen out of ink? Here's mine." I think many of those techniques are passed down without ever thinking about how they actually work—or don't work.

Securing commitment is one thing. You have to do it. But if you try to be a hard closer with the idea that somehow that's going to feel good to a customer, that won't be helpful.

Hard-charging closers are salespeople with high drive but lower empathy. If they had any empathy at all, they would see the signs that their closing approach make their customers feel uncomfortable.

If you are tempted to be a hard closer, you might look at whether modifying your approach might help you become more effective.

Hard closers are what give salespeople and selling a bad name. That bugs me. I am convinced that there are a lot of people who could be great salespeople but don't even consider it as a career option because they have been turned off by the stereotypical aggressive closer.

Ask for commitment? Absolutely! But resist becoming a hard-charging closer. It won't help you be more successful.

✎ LESSON 6 ✎

THE RESPONSIBILITY OF TRUST

I THINK THE WAY I APPROACH THINGS IS THAT I'M IN IT
FOR THE LONG HAUL. I DON'T NEED TO BE THE CLIENT'S
FRIEND. I DON'T REALLY WANT TO BE THE CLIENT'S
FRIEND, HONESTLY. BUT I WANT TO BE THE BEST PROFES-
SIONAL PARTNER THAT I CAN BE. I WANT THEM TO KNOW
THAT I CARE ABOUT THEIR BUSINESS.
—RHONDA KUHLMAN

I TALKED A LOT ABOUT PIERRE BOUVARD'S APPROACH TO
CUSTOMERS IN THE TEACH, DON'T SELL CHAPTER. But there
is one additional thing you should know about him. It's critical
to your understanding of Servant Heart Selling.

Pierre called on every single one of my competitors. He

would usually be seeing all of them on the same trip to town. Radio is a fiercely competitive business. Competitors were trying to take my audience, my advertisers, and especially my people. It was not a high-trust environment. There was so much I never wanted my competitors to know.

And yet I told Pierre my secrets. Within a short time of meeting him, I was pretty open about what was going on with our station. At some point, I even started to share some of the details of what was becoming a contentious time with my partners. I told him all that, knowing that he was going to leave my office and head immediately to one of my competitors.

Why didn't that make me nervous? It was because in all my dealings with Pierre, there was never any disclosure or a single bit of gossip about any of those same competitors. I became certain very early in our relationship that if he wasn't talking about them, he probably wasn't talking about me.

I trusted Pierre. As Jim Stoos says, "Trust and information have to be held sacred."

When a salesperson develops trust with a customer, that completely changes the game. For years, I used to say, "People buy from people they like." But there are lots of very likable people who aren't successful in sales. Today, I believe that people buy from people they *trust*. That is way more important than being liked.

Randy Mascagni manages people's money. And he thinks being trusted by his clients is huge: "I think it's a big deal, particularly when you're dealing with somebody's money. They certainly don't want to lose money. They want it to grow. The other thing is, they want to believe that they can share their situation, their life, and their information, and it's not going to travel down the road."

It's *all* about trust.

How Do You Get to Be Trusted?

You can't wave a magic wand and get a customer to trust you. You have to earn it. But that doesn't mean it has to take decades to achieve. Servant Heart Sellers can quickly get to a place where they are trusted by customers and prospects.

We all have some people we feel we can trust pretty quickly and some we'll never trust. How do they do successful sellers build trust? It's a combination of attitude and actions.

We can easily outline the action steps. Here are a few examples:

- You can start to build trust by being incredibly prepared for your first meeting with a customer. That's so different from what most sellers do that it quickly makes a positive statement about you.

- Being totally focused on their issues and challenges and not talking at all about your solutions in the initial discussions is very, very trust creating. Ask a million questions!

- Bill Gangloff spent time in our interview talking about how he handles the details of his work with a customer. Whether it is billing or proof of performance, Bill is meticulous about making sure everything is perfect. Because most of his competitors don't do that, his efforts make a real statement to the customer about how he is paying attention to their account.

- My friend Randy Watson was the king of sending articles. If you were an important client of Randy, you were likely to receive an article about something that was relevant to your business a couple of times per month. That small effort paid big dividends as clients saw Randy as completely different from other salespeople who called on them.

- Great sellers like Randy have shown me that what you do after you make that first sale (or two) is when you'll really demonstrate your commitment to the customer! If your customer has any sense that you have a "love them and leave them" attitude, you'll go backward. So actively staying in touch after you have made a sale is so very critical. Make sure those "touches" aren't just to stay in touch or be social and try to add value.

- Servant Heart Sellers are often suggesting options that are less expensive for the customer. Consultant AJ Vaden does that all the time. After spending time with a prospective client who had serious time issues, she suggested a lower-cost option that took way less time: "You could buy the bigger package. But after speaking to you, I am not sure you'd use it. This is what might work." That makes a huge statement to a customer.

- Tell the truth. I guess that should be obvious. But here's an example. I have a car repair place I trust. Why do I trust them? I took my car there a couple of years ago expecting a big problem. After checking it out, they told me it was just a tiny problem. They could have taken advantage of my lack of knowledge, but they didn't. And now I trust them completely.

"I Screwed Up"—How Servant Heart Sellers Build Trust by Dealing with Mistakes

Servant Heart Sellers deal with mistakes straight on. And they don't ever dodge responsibility. "If it happened in our building, it is my issue, not someone else's," says Bill Gangloff. "If I do make a mistake and there's some issue, I'll pick up the phone. You've got to be able to face it. You've got to be able to call them and say, 'Hey, look, we made a mistake.' I never pass the buck. I never say, 'Oh, my assistant put it in incorrectly.' Ultimately, that's my responsibility. You can't ever blame anyone for it."

Owning your mistakes is huge. When I was leading salespeople, I wanted to have people on our team who would admit their mistakes. There's a culture of blame that is pervasive in some quarters: "The dog ate my homework." It's a pet peeve of mine. I believe I have never met a truly successful person who was a blamer. They take responsibility.

Many people seem to think that admitting they made a mistake or don't know something is a sign of weakness. It's the opposite. Telling the customer (or even your boss) that you screwed up is a sign of strength. Sales superstars tend to be people who say "I screwed up." They own their mistakes.

They don't wait to get caught! Servant Heart Sellers admit

mistakes the customer may not even know about. They don't wait for problems to come to them. They are bringing things to the customer's attention immediately. We've all had the experience of having a company say, "Oh yeah, I was going to tell you about that." Doesn't that lead erode trust? What else haven't you told me? But if someone comes to you before you know there's an issue, that makes you confident they are paying attention. As Bill Gangloff says, "Being proactive leads to longevity." Don't ever forget. The easiest way to earn trust is to be completely trustworthy.

What Is the Opposite of Arrogance?

Some say the opposite of arrogance is meekness. That wouldn't fit with the great salespeople I know. They are not meek. And they are certainly not servile, another word the dictionary suggests.

I think the opposite of arrogance is humility.

Most people find it very hard to trust someone who comes across as arrogant. The know-it-all personality can be offensive. Lots of people are smart enough to know that. But their arrogance takes on another form. They are convinced they know the solution before they even understand the problem. That may be one of the most common mistakes salespeople make. Even if it's done in a gentle voice, it's arrogant.

As I wrote earlier, humility is a sales word. It means being humble enough to know what you don't know and being committed to listening to learn.

Being humble and being curious are qualities that seem to

be present in almost all the Servant Heart Sellers interviewed for this book. That's a big reason why they are able to build deep trust with their customers.

For Bill Gangloff, "Humility is a big part of what we do... it's not your wallet that's leading you but your desire and your heart and your mind to help that person. Not everybody wants to be helped or can be helped, but in a self-serving kind of fashion almost, I love to help. That makes me feel good."

The Incredible Responsibility of Trust

When you get to a point that a customer totally trusts you, that's wonderful. But you then have a moral obligation to make sure the advice you are giving or the product that you are selling really makes a difference for them.

And that's a big deal.

Oscar Mejia puts it very directly: "You cannot *try* with $100,000 of somebody else's money. You cannot try. You have to feel confident that what you do is what you suggest, and it has to work. If you don't, what is the point? So you don't trust money to someone just to try."

It has to work.

When AJ Vaden was selling expensive consulting projects to large companies like Verizon or Bridgestone Tire, she would suggest that a client begin small. She says, "My first step was always a research project, which was not what most people were used to. Most of them were used to some sort of service agreement." AJ says, "Let's not sign a twelve-month agreement until we have gone on some dates. So step one is we're going to date. My typical research projects were thirty to ninety days. We're going to date. You can take the deliverables from that and go hire someone else. I will not be offended."

AJ knew that if a client spent the time to put together an effective research project, it was highly unlikely they would choose anyone else for the implementation phase.

For other sellers, the responsibility required by trust means giving the customer straight advice even when that advice may not be in your best interest in the short term. Barbara Anderson had that experience several times in the earliest days of the COVID-19 lockdown. "I had three car dealers call and ask, 'What should I do?' And I got off on the phone, and I thought to myself they were asking me what I should do because they didn't know. Should I advertise? Should I not advertise? But I felt good because I was the person they trusted to call and give them a little bit of advice."

That kind of trust has to be treated with respect. There is big responsibility in having a client trust you like that.

If you are new to selling or want to take your game to the next level, here is the most direct advice you should hear: you *must* know your stuff. Knowing your stuff is *way* more than simple product knowledge. It's understanding the total picture.

For Jasmine Ruschmann and Meg Linne, who sell food products to major retailers, it's not just knowing their product. It's knowing the entire category their products compete in.

Dave Wall not only has to know the about motorhome coaches he sells, but he also has to intimately know the competitor's coaches. That's critical to him because his coaches are so much more expensive than his competitors'.

The investment advisers interviewed for this book feel

the responsibility of trust acutely. Al Fox said it well: "We are never satisfied with our own practice, meaning we continue to test assumptions. We continue to press to be innovative. We continue to build up our industry expertise. We have a lot of families that are counting on us to stay sharp, to stay energized, to stay well read and informed."

People who sell advertising can't just know the features of their own media or station. They have to know the marketing principles that drive results. They must have real expertise of how digital and traditional media work together. It's not enough to just know their own product. Not even close.

You are required to know your products at a deeper level. If a client comes to trust you, then they rely on you for advice just like Barbara Anderson's customers do. You honor that trust by being absolutely sure you give them advice that is good for their business. That's the responsibility of trust.

Servant Heart Sellers build amazing long-term relationships. But the goal isn't the relationship. The goal is *trust*. Trust is built when the solutions a salesperson provides exceeds the customer's expectations. Trust is the foundation. But when the trust you earned gets married with expertise, then the magic occurs. When you have earned trust and you bring expertise, your chances of holding on to that customer for a long, long time are very high.

The Servant Heart Sellers' Difference

As I mentioned, I used to tell salespeople in my sessions, "People buy from people they like." Today, I think that's wrong. Don't get me wrong, being liked isn't a bad thing. But it can't be your objective. Today, I believe that people buy from people they trust!

If you think it takes years to build trust with a client, you are wrong. It can happen quickly if you go into a call with an attitude of service, true humility, and being really prepared. Because that's so rare, you can build trust more quickly. But know this. If you can gain trust quickly, you can also lose it in a second.

When I started thinking about writing this book, I was afraid people would think it was about relationships more than sales effectiveness. I probably emphasize softer skills way more than a typical sales book. But following all the principles in this book will lead to greater success. And the foundation might just be building trust.

Highly effective reps have learned how to build trust early in the relationship. And that trust makes dealing with them a lot easier.

But trust brings with it an incredible responsibility. Customers need to know that your advice is not just your opinion but based on critical thinking and product knowledge that make your advice almost always lead to a solution that meets your customer's needs.

THE CUSTOMER IS NOT ALWAYS RIGHT

THE MOST IMPORTANT DECISION I MAKE EVERY YEAR IS
WHAT ACCOUNTS TO FIRE. —RANDY WATSON

IF YOU WERE ABLE TO BE INVISIBLE AND WATCH SERVANT
HEART SELLERS INTERACT WITH NEW AND EXISTING CUS-
TOMERS, THERE IS ONE PHRASE YOU WOULD HEAR A LOT.

You would hear them tell customer, "You could do that, but
..."

And they'd follow that with very specific reasons why what
the customer was thinking about doing may not be the best
approach to take.

"You could do that, but ..."

There are way too many salespeople who are so anxious to

close a sale that they say yes to customers when they should say *no*. They get the satisfaction of making a sale. Maybe their boss even gives them a high five. They earn a commission. But if what they sold that customer doesn't solve the customer's problem, then the seller is likely "one and done." Because Servant Heart Sellers are playing the long game, they want customers for years, not months. For them to take a deal that gets them a sale but doesn't really do the job for the customer isn't just bad business; it is morally wrong.

Dean Thibault, executive vice president of Landmark National Bank, takes that attitude and has made it part of the business development culture for their commercial bankers.

"The worst thing we can do is develop a sale and then find out later that it's not a good fit. We aren't for everybody. Part of that is humility. We're not a good fit, and that's just fine. We can't take care of everybody, but we know what we can deliver and what we're all about. For those clients who see the value in it, it's a long-term relationship that doesn't break."

That attitude—we have to be a good fit—changes the way Dean's people will respond. And it gives them permission to walk away from business that they don't feel is good long-term fit for the bank.

Let's look at another example. It comes from my media experience. I'll ask the sellers at a TV station this question: "How much does a new client have to spend per month for their first three months to absolutely know your products work?" Every station I have ever worked with has a consensus answer to that question. They might say, "The customer needs to spend $5,000 per month for three months," and if they do, they will see measurable results.

What happens if the customer only wants to spend $1,500 per month? I don't know if this true in your industry, but in ours, about 80 percent of the sellers would take that order. Some might even get in trouble with their boss if they didn't take it because there is so much pressure to grow new business.

They may think they have won in the short term. After all, they made a sale. Isn't that what salespeople are supposed to do? They have made a sale, but what they sold that client won't likely produce a lot of results for their customer. Is that good business? I hope you are saying *no*. Servant Heart Sellers would *never* take that business. Remember the adage "What's good for the customer will ultimately be good for you"? Well, the opposite is true as well. If it's *not* good for the customer, it will ultimately not be good for you either. So it's in your best interest to say no.

Saying no is not easy. It's especially not easy if you are a commission salesperson with some financial pressures. Many of us have taken deals we should have not taken because of some financial stress. I can list some I've been part of for sure. It takes courage to walk away when we "need" the business. And yet if we are truly committed to be a Servant Heart Seller, we have to do that.

But there's good news. Keep reading.

Walk Away to Win

Servant Heart Sellers say, "You could do that, but . . . "

They also often tell customers that a competitor probably would sell them what they want way but that they won't. What a message that sends to a customer when you turn down the chance to make a sale.

Servant Heart Sellers say *no*. They say no to existing customers who have ideas that don't make sense. And they especially say no to new clients. Every bone in your body may want to say yes. But if you say yes to something that's not right for the customer, you have likely hurt them and hurt yourself.

Servant Heart Sellers know that when they say *no*, that single act can change the dynamic of the relationship and help create even more trust with their clients.

When you say no, it makes a huge statement that 1) you know what you are doing, 2) you have a plan you are very confident will work, and 3) you are prepared to walk away rather than do something that isn't in your customer's best interest.

Does saying no immediately lead to yes? Unfortunately, that's not always the case. Some customers may not believe your ideas. Others believe but don't have the money to do things in a way the seller thinks is right. But every Servant Heart Seller would tell you that many, many times in their career, saying no has quickly led to a selling plan that does work for the client. There will sometimes be a modest compromise. But Servant Heart Sellers never take a deal they believe to be bad for the customer.

What Is the Lifetime Value of Your Customer?

There's a study that says that the lifetime value of a Taco Bell customer is $11,000. Those $5 purchases do up over time. So what happens when someone has a bad experience at Taco Bell? It's like watching $11,000 walk out the door.

Smart businesses look at lifetime customer value all the time. It helps them know how much they can spend to acquire a customer. Or how they may invest to serve a customer better and therefore create more loyalty.

Lifetime customer value can be huge. Think about Dave Wall. He's had customers who have bought multiple coaches from him. He told he's had some customers who have bought as many as eight or nine from him. These coaches aren't cheap. And even though he has a huge repeat business, there are a few folks who may only buy one. But if you average out all his customers, the lifetime value could be as high as $5 million or more. That's a lot of money represented by each client.

So what if Dave sold them something that wasn't right for them in his first transaction? Say goodbye to $5 million.

Most salespeople don't ever think about lifetime customer value when they are making their first sale to a client. All they think about is the value of that sale and the commission they will earn. And frankly, we set up commission plans and sales contests that frequently reward the one-time sale and not any long-term business.

When you start to calculate the lifetime value of a customer, one thing gets very clear: saying no to situations that create no opportunity for a lifetime customer is good business.

What is the lifetime value of your customer? Is it close to Taco Bell's $11,000 or Liberty Coach's $5 million? Or, like most of us, somewhere in between? Whatever the number is, you can be clear on one very important idea. You'll lose any opportunity to have a long-term customer relationship if you don't sell the client the right thing from the beginning. You think you have lost just one sale. But the impact on your revenue is so much more than that.

When you say no and are prepared to walk away, you sometimes get a win right away from a client who respects the strengths of your convictions. But you always win in the long term as you turn more clients from "one and done" into long-term relationships.

Firing Customers

Salespeople are always focused on making a sale, right? So it seems heretical to suggest that sometimes one of the best things you can do is end your relationship with a customer.

But strong salespeople do that all the time. Often, it's at the beginning of the relationship when it's clear that it's not a good fit. That's what was outlined above.

But sellers who maintain a book of business will often decide that moving on from a client can be an absolutely great business decision.

Randy Watson, who was one of my smart teachers as a seller, told me that the most important decision he would make each year was what accounts to fire. By fire he didn't mean bringing them in and offering a severance package—"You're fired!" Randy worked with his managers to get another salesperson to handle that customer so the company didn't lose the business.

So why would Randy want to give up the commission from any piece of business? The answer was he'd done the math. If you take your earnings for the year and divide it by the number of weeks you work, you can quickly calculate your projected hourly wage. This is a great exercise.

If you project you'll earn $100,000 this year, that means you are making $2,000 per week or about $50 per hour. So what if a customer takes four hours per month of your time but only earns you $100 in commission? When the gap between your time and your commission is significant, it doesn't make sense to keep them, especially when skilled sellers are confident they could use that four hours per month to find a bigger, more profitable opportunity to work with. And that's the key idea. Servant Heart Sellers know that their biggest asset is their time. So they don't want to waste time with low-potential customers.

The sales managers who are reading this are probably thinking, *Well, they could get bigger.* And if there's a good chance of that, don't fire them. At least, not yet! Continue to work with them to see if that potential becomes reality. Top sellers don't just hope that happens. They often think of themselves as running their own business. Because they feel that way and know their big asset is their time, they'll make realistic judgements about when a client isn't going to grow to a point that makes sense for them to handle.

Randy may also fire a client if he can't get comfortable with the way they do business. In the media business, salespeople almost always have responsibilities to collect receivables from the customer. So Randy may fire a customer if they constantly needed to be chased for money.

But there's a more common reason Servant Heart Sellers would "fire" a client. Because they are so committed to making a difference for their customers, they can get frustrated when they want results for the customer more than the customer wants it for themselves. When you want it for them more than they want it for themselves, you may decide that's a relationship that isn't good for either side.

Let's add some realism to this section. This advice won't apply to every salesperson who reads this book. For PepsiCo's Meg Linne or RXBAR's Jasmine Ruschmann, it's completely unrealistic to say fire a client. They, like so many sellers, have either a territory they are responsible for or a huge national customer they work with exclusively. You also won't fire a client who makes up a huge percentage of your income even if they are complete jerks.

The big issue is how you are going to use your time. If you spend all your time chasing smaller deals and working with clients who aren't as committed to results as you are, you'll squander time and opportunities to really grow your business and work with customers who truly have the potential to be long-term partners. One of the smartest things I have ever read was written by Democratic political strategists Paul Begala and James Carville in their book about the Clinton campaign, *Buck Up, Suck Up... and Come Back When You Foul Up*. Don't worry, this is a truly bipartisan quote because it was originally said by Republican House Speaker Newt Gingrich:

A lion is fully capable of capturing, killing, and eating a field mouse. But it turns out that the energy required to do so exceeds the caloric content of the mouse itself. So a lion that spent its day hunting and eating field mice would slowly starve to death. A lion can't live on field mice. A lion needs antelope.

Antelope are big animals. They take more speed and strength to capture and kill, and once killed, they provide a feast for the lion and her pride. A lion can live a long and happy life on a diet of antelope.

The distinction is important. Are you spending all your time and exhausting all your energy catching field mice?

In the short term, it may give you a nice, rewarding feeling. But in the long run, you're going to die. So ask yourself at the end of the day, "Did I spend today chasing mice or hunting antelope?"

If you're honest with yourself and the answer is mice, you'd better reassess your focus, get back to the strategic core, and get your butt on the trail of an antelope.

Why should you consider firing clients? To free up more of your time to chase antelopes.

The Servant Heart Sellers' Difference

Most salespeople are afraid to push back on a customer. They think disagreement might cost them a sale. Nothing could be further from the truth. I am not suggesting you have to argue or be a jerk. No raising of voices here. We are partners with our customers. But if a customer has an idea that doesn't make sense, I feel like I have a responsibility to politely disagree.

There's an obligation that is inherent in this. Do you know what you are talking about? Because Servant Heart Sellers become experts in their product and how it works, they can push back. It's important to have that expertise. Otherwise, you are expressing an opinion that may or may not be based on actual customer experience.

Some of the best relationships in my selling career came out of situations where I respectfully disagreed.

Servant Heart Sellers feel an obligation to push back if they feel a customer is heading in the wrong direction.

ᔥ LESSON 8 ᕁ

ABOVE AND BEYOND
SELLING

PRICE IS WHAT YOU PAY. VALUE IS WHAT YOU GET.
—WARREN BUFFETT

REMEMBER MY STORY OF OSCAR PICKING UP TRASH IN THE
PARKING LOT AT HIS CUSTOMERS' BIG EVENT?

His radio station was broadcasting live at a client, and he
was out in the parking lot picking up trash and straightening
out the shopping carts. Or how about Mattress Mac at Gallery
Furniture going on Facebook Live during Hurricane Harvey? He
had trucks that could rescue people but didn't have any drivers.
So, he told the community via Facebook that he needed some

drivers. They showed up and brought hundreds of stranded people to his stores, where they stayed.

Turns out that when you talk to Servant Heart Sellers, those kinds of things aren't even particularly unusual. It's part of their DNA. When I asked Mattress Mac about what he did during Harvey, it was almost like it was no big deal. "These are my people," he said. "What else would I do?"

Servant Heart Sellers add tremendous value and create incredible loyalty by doing more for their customers than their competitors. They do things for customers usually with little thought that make a huge statement. And the impact can be huge.

Earlier in this book, I shared my personal experience as a client of Pierre Bouvard, who represented the Arbitron ratings service. There is one other part of my experience with him that totally changed our relationship. It happened right at the beginning.

Just two weeks after we had bought the radio station, I was heading to New York City with my partner to meet our brand-new rep firm. Rep firms represent stations like ours to big national advertisers with New York ad agencies, and I wanted to make a big impression on them. Earlier in the week before, I had shared with Pierre that I was making this trip. My memory is fuzzy about whether we had even met at that point, but we had definitely spoken on the phone.

Saturday morning at eleven o'clock, the doorbell rang at my home in Rochester. It was a FedEx delivery from Pierre. Inside were four graphs he had created that demonstrated why our new format change made sense for the Rochester market, graphs that would make the case to all the folks at the rep firm in a way that would really be helpful.

I remember saying, "*Wow.*" And I remember my partner, Steve Chartrand, who had lots and lots of years dealing with Arbitron, wondering if he could get Pierre for his rep at his station in the northeast.

Pierre made a huge statement to me. And for him, just like for Mattress Mack, it was completely natural.

My first book for advertising salespeople was called *Don't Just Make a Sale, Make a Difference.* The title came from a lunch with a broadcaster whom I really admired, Milt Maltz. Milt was likely a billionaire because of his success in the radio and TV business. But he never forgot his beginnings as a salesperson in a weak AM radio station in a Detroit suburb. His lunch comment? He said, "The problem with our business today is that we don't have enough salespeople who understand their job is to make a difference in the lives of their customers." In other words, it's not just about the product you sell. The real goal is to make a difference for our customers. That is a concept that Servant Heart Sellers totally understand.

Most bankers have loan officers. But Landmark National Bank calls them commercial bankers, *not* commercial lenders. Dean Thibault argues that the difference isn't just in the words. Bankers see themselves as looking at the entire picture of a customer's business. Lenders just want to sell a loan.

Dean shared a little of the Landmark philosophy: "It's about bringing up this common culture among our commercial bankers that goes beyond just lending. It's really uncovering what the other things we can do to help the business succeed. We deal with businesses day in and day out, and what we're willing to do is share what we've learned from other clients and customers, in confidence certainly, and making referrals and making suggestions and introductions and all those kinds of things."

As the trust builds, Landmark's bankers start to become true partners with the business they serve.

Deans says, "We're in a position where we can say, 'Let's put together a plan.' What's more, if you've got a potential buyer or someone that's in the business that might be interested, let's talk to them early. Let's develop this. That's been tremendously successful for us. That's just an example of what we do."

Helping a business think about a possible exit strategy, even meeting with a potential buyer, is above and beyond the normal lender relationship. Is that powerful? Well, I can tell you that I have owned businesses for over forty years, and I have never had a conversation like that with any of the bankers I have ever dealt with. I hung up from my interview with Dean Thibault wishing that Landmark had a branch in Florida. That's because the difference between the approach he described and the banks I have worked with could not be more dramatic. As a business owner, I have dealt with some of the biggest banks in the country. They could learn a whole lot about taking care of customers from Dean.

Many, many times, the above and beyond things have little to do with the specific product you sell.

Mortgage broker Jeff Wagner consciously wants to be a bigger resource to the realtors who refer business to him. "I want to be the go-to guy for not just business, but other things like where's a good place to volunteer, where to get your haircut. Anything. I want to do as much of that as possible."

And remember, Jeff does ten times the volume of most successful brokers do every month. He's a giver. It's part of his

DNA. So of course he wants to serve.

For Jeff, it's about giving without keeping score. He says, "I think that's where most people go wrong. They give and they expect something. That's very shortsighted, and that's a tough place to be. I was unintentionally doing that years ago. When it was a weight lifted off my shoulder. Now I don't have those feelings of 'How am I going to benefit?'"

That idea of not keeping score is so hard, especially for a group of driven salespeople who like to win. Servant Heart Sellers seem to have a belief in karma. Give it away, and it will come back to you. You never know how (or when) it will come back to you, but Servant Heart Sellers have a strong belief it will.

How can you go above and beyond? There will be different things in different industries. Introducing a couple of your customers who may be able to work together or even just connect as friends may work. Jeff Wagner has formalized that and has a group of his referral partners to his home for a great dinner.

David Melville gives away books. I remember talking about certain books in a seminar, and within days, David had read it himself. If he found the book valuable, he would buy more copies and give them to customers he thought might get value from it. I love to give away books. Many of my clients have the same drive to learn that I have. When I discover we share that drive and I send them a book, I feel like it adds some glue to our relationship. Bill Gangloff asks if he can come to a client's sales meeting to learn more about their business. That's glue being added.

Helping a customer solve other business issues is huge. Suppose you were calling on a client, and they told you they had sales challenges. Could you think about maybe conducting a sales meeting for them that might help? What would doing that say to your client? And how much glue would that add to your relationship?

This is not about coffee mugs and tickets.

My dad worked in purchasing and purchasing management for some very big companies. He didn't always have a great opinion about the men who called on him. (And in those days, it was *always* men!) I suspect that to his dying day, he could not understand why his son got into sales. And then I even started training salespeople. Talk about damaging the family name!

In my dad's time, it was not uncommon for salespeople to try to use gifts in ways that almost seemed like bribery. When I was in my teens, I remember a salesman who called on my dad dropping off a case of great scotch right before Christmas. My dad loved good scotch. But he had my mother call the salesman and tell him to come back and take the scotch back. That always impressed me.

Today's sellers know that those kind of things won't work. It's even prohibited conduct for most companies, prohibited for both buyers to offer and sellers to accept. So sellers today try to do little things, small gifts that say thank you to the client.

There's nothing wrong with offering tickets or taking a client to lunch. But you need to be aware that if all your competitors have access to food and tickets, then food and tickets will never be a differentiator. This is so important to understand. If your competitors have the same things as you do, that won't make a difference. It won't even make a statement. Again, there is nothing wrong with doing these things. But just don't have any expectations about how they will help you. They usually don't.

Smart sellers use those tools differently. What if those tickets became the basis of a sales contest you helped your client to create? Or were used to help that customer entertain one of their key clients? Or their kids? I will never forget the rep who took my dad and me sailing on Long Island Sound. He gave my very busy dad the gift of time with his son. Surely more powerful than a couple of tickets to a ball game!

In the course of the interviews for this book, I heard countless examples of this above and beyond service, everything from recommending a barber to helping a client's daughter get an internship. For Servant Heart Sellers, this is never about a quid pro quo. No "You wash my back, and I'll wash yours." They usually don't keep score. They just give and serve. They stop keeping score because they believe that if they give, they will get back.

The Servant Heart Sellers' Difference

There's a big question in this chapter. Is this natural or learned behavior? I've made my living as a trainer, so it won't surprise you that I think people can change. Here's what I guess happens when it comes to going above and beyond, and I think it is what happened to me. My instincts were to serve. And as I followed those instincts, I discovered that it deepened my relationship with customers, which made me more comfortable being more consistent that way.

I also think sellers have to be careful that how they go above and beyond adds real value. A TV rep I know has a client who wants a weekly planning meeting with her and her competitors. And yet the amount he spends doesn't justify the amount of time she spends with him. I sure hope she would not read this and think I would endorse that use of her time.

Here is another thought: in seminars about giving *wow* customer service, they also talk about "random and unexpected," like the time I got a note from the Delta pilot thanking me for being a two-million-mile Delta flier. I am guessing Oscar's picking up trash is so unexpected that he gets a lot more credit than other actions may earn him.

Let's be honest. Most salespeople don't do this. It's not on their radar at all. And that's a big reason why the impact of being an above and beyond seller is so huge.

NEVER STOP LEARNING

It's what you learn after you know it all that really counts. —Coach John Wooden

Here's the scene: I'm invited to Des Moines, Iowa, to speak to a group of car dealers about marketing their dealerships. As is often the case, I got to have dinner the night before with a local dealer. This night, it was a man named Stew Hansen. I was excited to meet him because at that time, Stew owned one of the most successful Dodge-Chrysler dealerships in the entire country. I already knew him by reputation. I love getting to hang out with successful people (more on that later), so I was very psyched.

Stew was at the age where he was thinking about how to transition his business. During dinner, Stew shared privately with me that he had recently turned down the chance to sell his stores for a huge amount of money. We talked briefly about all the challenges of making a decision like that. A few years later, he did indeed sell his dealerships to the Garff family.

Stew was hugely successful, rich by all material standards. He was near the end of his career. But guess where he was at seven thirty the next morning. He was sitting in the front row of my seminar, taking page after page of notes. And it was no surprise he was the first person to approach me after the session, asking for additional information about something I had shared.

Stew Hansen represents something I believe in strongly. Successful people never stop learning. And you see that, big time, in the way Servant Heart Sellers approach their businesses.

It's simple. If you are driven to serve your clients, you can't ever stop learning because your lack of knowledge about something may reduce your ability to make a difference. For investment adviser Al Fox, it's a drive to continue to be "world class" in what he does that drives that need to continue to learn.

Earlier, we wrote about humility being the opposite of arrogance. And it is beyond arrogant to think you know it all. I'll confess that one of my absolute pet peeves is someone who sits in a seminar all day and doesn't take a single note. If you are doing that in one of my sessions, please know I will be judging you! Servant Heart Sellers are the opposite of that. They, like Stew Hansen, are often the ones taking the most notes. And they'll be the first to challenge something they want clarity about or need to talk about further. Barbara Anderson says that, for her part, "as you get older, you get more clear about what you *don't* know."

Al Fox made me laugh when he told me that the person who graduated first in their med school class at Harvard and the person who graduated last in their med school class at some less-than-Harvard medical school both call themselves doctors. And I'm guessing that you don't want to go to a doctor who doesn't keep up with the latest medical journals and research about their specialty.

When I was an up-and-coming speaker, one of the biggest names in the speaking business was Charlie "Tremendous" Jones. Jones was a motivational speaker who knew that success wasn't just about a positive attitude. His most famous saying was "You will be the same person in five years as you are today except for the people you meet and the books you read."

We learn from books we read and the people we meet. So it's important to be deliberate about your choices in both.

So I ask you . . . who are your teachers?

When JDA's Jim Stoos speaks about the difference between being confident and being egotistical, he's clear that confidence comes by his continuing to be a student: "I'm confident in what I'm doing. I'm confident that I can help you. That doesn't mean that I'm egotistical, though. We can talk about ourselves too long, and always we look like we have high egos, not confidence. I don't know how many books I read. At least a dozen, if not twenty, a year, not to mention webinars. I have two digital teachers who I trust to educate me as well." He, like all the Servant Heart Sellers I interviewed, never stops learning. Barbara Anderson told me, "I used to have a notebook in my office, and I would write down one thing I learned new about somebody, about life, business, anything. I learned something new today, and here it is."

Investment adviser Al Fox says, "We continue to want to be

world class in what we do." When you have that as a goal, you can't stop learning and thinking about how you might get better.

As I was writing this section, I laughed. Does it seem silly that I am writing about the importance of continuous learning to readers who are deep into a book? Talk about preaching to the choir! But here's the challenge for all of us today: technology has provided all of us with more information than ever. A quick Google search of any topic gives you more opportunities to go down a rabbit hole of information than at any point in history. There are five million results to the query "pivoting your business during COVID." The problem isn't finding places to spend your reading time. The challenge today is to make sure you are reading the right things. It's possible today that there may be more knowledge and less learning than ever. So being conscious of what you are consuming and certain it's helping you get better is essential now.

Some specifics:

Read every bestselling business book that you think may impact, even tangentially, what you sell. Busy or spending lots of car time? Audible is amazing. The legendary Zig Ziglar called the car "your university on wheels." I know a lot of great salespeople who use their driving time well.

As an entrepreneur, I love to read books about how successful entrepreneurs have built their companies. I find them thought-provoking and inspiring.

There are lots and lots of good leadership content on LinkedIn. Become a thirty-second reader. Give yourself permission to bail out of any article after thirty seconds if you don't think it will help you. Become a very discriminating reader.

You must expand your knowledge of business in general. I

read the *Wall Street Journal* for years before I had much money to invest. Today, I spend time each day on a couple of the financial news websites. I read articles about how companies are dealing with challenges or going after new opportunities.

Take classes and seminars. One of my good friends joined Toastmasters because she felt that improving her communication skills was something she needed to work on. Legendary investor Warren Buffett says the absolute best investment you can make is on yourself. Servant Heart Sellers know that!

The old cliché says knowledge is power. Actually, I think that's wrong. Knowledge combined with action is power. But Servant Heart Sellers are committed to learning because they know that knowledge can be a differentiator between them and their competition.

One word of caution: knowledge isn't just about what you know about your product. I can know more about TV advertising than anyone in America. But that's not even close to what I need to know to truly serve a client. Besides the knowledge of the product I sell, I need to know marketing strategy principles. I need to know the strengths and weaknesses of my competitors. I must have a clear understanding of which digital tools are best for specific business challenges. Understanding how advertising impacts profitability and the critical importance of market share is essential. And those are just some of the things on the list.

That's my list. What does a similar list look like for the product you sell? Do you sell insurance or investments? To truly be knowledgeable in your field, what do you need to know about? The list will be way more than just a clearer understanding of the specs of what you sell.

The Gift of Mentors

Charlie "Tremendous" Jones says it's not just the books. It's also the people you meet who will help you to continue to grow. Servant Heart Sellers can almost always identify people who are their teachers.

Mentors are significant to becoming a lifelong learner. The first three bosses I had were critical to my success. What I learned from each of them early in my career continues to impact me to this day. One of them, a car dealer, literally modeled for me what success looked like. He convinced me that successful people got up early in the morning. Today, I'm not even sure if that's true. But it's been my personal habit ever since I came to know him. And that was a long time ago.

Each of my first three mentors loved to teach. Each of them gave me the incredible gift of their time! I wonder if leaders and managers today who try to manage people and answer sixty or one hundred emails per day have the time to make that commitment of time. Most leaders are already crazy busy. But we need mentors more than ever. I know how important my three teachers were to my career. But I fear that those same three people might have been buried in emails or corporate conference calls if they had been my bosses today. How much would I have missed if that was the case?

Some companies are dealing with those issues by having formal mentoring relationships. That's the case with the company my daughter Cassie works for, Rising Tide, a digital marketing agency. That's huge. But I am guessing it is also pretty unusual. Most of us are on our own. That's why it's important for you to consciously try to pick out people you think can help you.

Mentoring doesn't necessarily have to be a long-term relationship. I've learned powerful lessons from people I sought out for a phone call or coffee. Most people find that the words "Can I pick your brain about X?" are pretty effective at getting even extremely busy people to give you some time. Of course, there is a responsibility in that. You can't waste their time. You must know the purpose of your discussion in advance. And be sure to formally say thank you after you have spent time with them. Being grateful for what they have given you keeps the door open for future discussions.

And be mindful of who you spend your time with. Lots of different people have said, "You are the average of the five people you spend the most time with." It's like this. If you want to be a better golfer, play golf with people who are better than you are. You won't get to be a better golfer by hanging out with me. If you want to be more successful, hang out with successful people! And ask them a million questions!

Many superstars have a group of people they call on for professional advice. I am privileged to be a member of several people's personal board of directors. Having something like that can also be a real difference maker for you.

The Learning Never Stops

Warren Buffett often shares that one of the foundations of his life is his commitment to learning. He says his goal is to go to bed each day "a little bit smarter." And he feels that knowledge is like investing. The real growth occurs through compounding. The knowledge you acquire today compounds over time. And the result is that you are more and more prepared to be great at what you do. So you never stop. You never stop because your desire to serve your customers means you must know everything you can that can make a difference.

Al Fox introduced me to the teachings of West Point instructor Tom Magnus. Magnus said, "You do not deserve to call yourself a professional unless you read and write daily." Al Fox said that after Magnus said that, he paused for a moment. And then he went on to say, "The reason I paused is I have to remind myself of that every day because it's hard to read and write every day. I didn't say write a novel. I didn't say read a novel. Read and write about your profession every day."

Great advice!

The Servant Heart Sellers' Difference

I have a strong belief that a commitment to lifelong learning is one of the most important ingredients of successful people. I'm seventy years old, and I am still learning. Since I decided to write this book, I attended a two-day seminar on launching a book and bought (and listened to) another audio program. Plus, I've found two advisers who are helping me. One of my mentors suggested a book that might be helpful, and I downloaded it. I hope I never stop being like this. I love the line "You are either growing or going." All of us, no matter our age, have to stay relevant in times that are changing so quickly.

If the world is changing and you are staying the same, you are actually going backward. And you'll pay for that pretty quickly. So here's the question. What are you reading and learning about today? Commit to being a lifelong learner!

REFUSE TO BE A COMMODITY

YOU KNOW YOU'VE DONE A GREAT JOB WHEN YOUR
CUSTOMER FORCE BECOMES YOUR SALES FORCE. IF
YOU'RE DOING THIS COMBATIVE "DEMOLITION MAN"
SELLING, THAT NEVER HAPPENS BECAUSE YOU'VE WON
AND THEY'VE LOST. SO EVEN THOUGH YOU'VE WON THE
BATTLE, YOU'VE LOST THE WAR. —RORY VADEN

AS YOU LOOK AT THE SERVANT HEART SELLING PILLARS we
have already outlined, you get a picture of why these stars have
such strong relationships with customers.

They are totally committed to customer outcomes even if it
is not always the best for them personally.

They are reluctant to sell something they don't believe is in the best interest of their customers.

They are constantly asking diagnosis questions to learn even more about their customers.

They push back on client requests and ideas when they believe they don't make sense.

They refuse to be hard-charging closers. They don't need to because they have spent a lot of time working on the right plan.

They are committed to learning. They are driven to learn anything that may help them be more effective for their customers.

What makes Servant Heart Sellers so valuable to their customers? You get *them*! It's not just the product that they sell you. You get *them*!

That's why folks with these selling skills are less impacted by price negotiations than other sellers. Notice that I didn't say that they weren't impacted at all. That would be naïve. But price becomes less of an issue when the product isn't the only thing the customer gets.

The Value = Price Equation

There is a fundamental equation that drives every buying decision. Value = price means that the customer will never pay you more than their perception of the value.

Think about a great steak at a restaurant. How much is that worth to you? Would you pay $30? Maybe more?

But let's take the same steak dinner and change the value equation. Suppose I told you that the restaurant is considered one of the most romantic in the country. You'll have a view of the Manhattan skyline at night and a view of the Statute of Liberty from your table. The service would be world class, and the dinner would be the final night of a wonderful trip to New York with the person you love the most. How much would you pay for that steak dinner now?

That steak, with an appetizer, salad, and dessert, is currently on the menu of the River Café for $130. Per person! The River Café has an amazing location on the East River, directly across from Lower Manhattan. I've been there twice, and both times were magical nights. I had no feelings that I had paid too much.

What did the River Café do to that steak dinner? They added value, lots of value. And they got paid for it.

Most salespeople don't have a world-class view of the skyline to add to their value. But Servant Heart Sellers avoid being a commodity by personally adding lots and lots of value to their clients. In fact, their entire selling approach is about adding value! Doing that effectively helps them from being in a bidding war that is totally focused on price.

Brian Richmond said that when he was new to selling insurance, he thought it was all about the price. Brian says, "When I first started out, I just wanted to make a sale. I remember going to Certified Insurance Counselor classes. The speaker would say, 'It's not about price,' and I'd think, 'You are full of crap! You're crazy.' I'm twenty-three years old, and I'm thinking it's absolutely about price." The Servant Heart Selling approach Brian uses today takes the emphasis away from price. He says, "I'll have a meeting with a client, go through things, and present it, and they say, 'That's great. Let's move forward.' They start to get up and leave, and the client says, 'Wait a minute, what does it cost?'" Because of Brian's sales approach, price becomes secondary. Brian adds value. And value makes price less significant.

There's a big difference between how the transactional seller and the Servant Heart Seller manages the value = price equation in the sales process. The Servant Heart Seller is totally focused on adding to the value side of the equation. The transactional seller doesn't have that option. That leaves them only one option. They have to lower the price to their client's perception of the value. Or they have to give something away with their product that makes it cheaper.

Too many salespeople think that the only way to manage the value = price equation is to lower the price. Servant Heart Sellers clearly know there are two sides to that equation. Long before there is any negotiation, these sellers have worked on the value side. They add value because they become more valuable to the customer. They are more valuable because of their expertise, their idea, their commitment. They add value over and over again.

Does This Make Sense?

The Discipline of Market Leaders, written by Michael Treacy and Fred Wiersema, is a book that has always made ton of sense to me. It says that market leaders usually hang their hat on one of the following three attributes.

Attribute 1: Price. Think Walmart.
Attribute 2: Customer service. Nordstrom or Ritz-Carlton are the examples that everyone may use.
Attribute 3: Technological innovation. How about Amazon for this one?

The book made a point that is very relevant here. It said that even if you staked your claim on one attribute, you cannot ignore the others. I might pay Nordstrom $10 more for the same shirt because of the ideas and service I get from a great salesperson. But I won't pay them $50 more for the shirt.

That idea is consistent with the experience of most of us in sales. If I have built an amazing relationship with a customer and they see me as trusted partner, they will pay me a little more for the product I sell. It likely won't be 50 percent more. Probably way less than that. But more.

Servant Heart Sellers will tell you that as long as they continue to create real value for their customers, they receive a powerful benefit. They are way less likely to be shopped at renewal. Make no mistake: if a customer finds out they are paying a whole lot more to buy from you, your great relationship won't be enough. But Servant Heart Sellers are able to charge a little more, have less price negotiation, and retain clients longer because they are constantly adding to the value side of the value = price equation.

The Dreaded Purchasing Agent

Many of us who sell do some our business with buyers whose job is focused on buying it for less. That might even be a lot of your business. Whether these people work in purchasing or are media buyers for an ad agency, their role is to pay less. Pepsi-Co's Meg Linne and RXBAR's Jasmine Ruschmann spend their time selling to buyers who work for huge national companies or grocery chains. That's a low margin business where every penny counts. So those buyers have a mandate to push hard to make the best deals.

How does the idea of not being a commodity work with buyers whose job requires them to make the decisions largely on price?

I think Meg and Jasmine would tell you that they feel there are still major advantages to establishing relationships of trust with their buyers. Both of them focus on working with customers on promotions that may spur sales at a particular chain. That can create a huge win for both parties. Every seller who calls on those chains wants a piece of that action. But those who have built a relationship of trust tend to get their ideas heard. That's a huge win.

They also have an advantage when there is a problem. Problems occur in all business relationships. A delivery is late, or a closing gets delayed. The commercials run in the wrong time period. Billing gets screwed up. When problems occur, the seller who has built a strong, trusting relationship can minimize the danger to the business relationship that the problem has caused.

Want proof of that idea? There's research that ties the frequency of malpractice suits against doctors to the amount of time that the doctor spends getting to know the patient. Doctors who are all business get sued more often. Doctors who demonstrate empathy and have a good bedside manner have less lawsuits. Patients like those doctors. And if you like your doctor, you are less likely to charge off to their lawyer when something goes wrong. The relationship creates a different environment for dealing with problems. It's the same for customers. When the customer trusts you, they are way more likely to work with you to deal with a problem when it occurs.

But perhaps the biggest advantage that Servant Heart Sellers have with that price-focused buyer is that they get information. Because they have such a strong relationship, the buyer can share insights on the company's strategy that can be helpful for the salesperson to plan future interactions. They also get information about competitors. Often buyers will give them clear guidance about what they need to do to make sure they secure a piece of business. Yes, price is still going to be important to these buyers. But your efforts to become more valuable and to build trust can pay huge dividends. And that makes it worth the time.

Don't Be a Commodity

Brian Richmond told me he does not even like to do a quote for a business that announces they "shop" their insurance every three years. Over the years, I have met several ad sellers who have decided they don't want to handle any advertising agencies because they don't like the transactional nature of that business. Plus, in media sales, that business usually pays a lot lower commission.

Landmark National Bank's Dean Thibault says, "I guess I would say that we don't compete with anyone. I know that may sound glib, but we're primarily interested in doing our thing."

We live in a world where more and more things are treated like commodity, and some would have you believe that price is the *only* thing that counts. Servant Heart Sellers would disagree. They are constantly focused on adding value to change the value = price equation. While most sellers pay attention to the price side, these great communicators work also on the value side.

Perhaps Liberty Coach's Dave Wall put it best: "People can buy a Chevy Caprice, or they can buy a Bentley or Rolls-Royce. They do the same thing, but they're not the same."

It's not just about price. Servant Heart Sellers never forget that.

The Servant Heart Sellers' Difference

It's really simple. Many salespeople get treated like they or their product is a commodity because they haven't really added any value. Avoiding being a commodity is, in many ways, the entire message and purpose of this book. Here's a simple truth. Until a salesperson figures out ways to deepen the relationship and add significant value, they will risk being seen as a commodity. And it does not have to be that way!

A Caveat: A Desire to Serve Won't Be Enough!

There are basic characteristics you must possess to be successful in sales. Companies spend millions of dollars each year to determine if sales candidates possess those traits. If you don't have them, you likely won't find much success selling. You can have the biggest heart in the world. You can be a person with a huge desire to serve. And you won't likely be successful without some fundamental traits. But if you have those characteristics *and* you add the principles in this book, you will be hugely successful. As Peter McCampbell, owner of Human Capital Metrics, says,

"It's a combination of flavors that makes a good salesperson."

Every sales attribute test I've ever seen tries to determine the level of drive a candidate possesses. A salesperson with no drive will find it hard to make the calls. The test McCampbell uses, PXT select, measures an individual's cognitive abilities or thinking styles, behaviors, and interests. McCampbell believes that the attribute they call "enterprising" is critical to being a successful seller. They also measure what they call "people service," an attribute Servant Heart Sellers would almost always possess. But McCampbell suggests that if you don't have enterprising, the strength of your people service may not be enough. That's because without that drive, "you may not speak up when the customer doesn't want to hear the perfect solution that they need to hear." McCampbell adds, "Enterprising is the belief you have the right to change someone's mind."

Is high drive enough? According to McCampbell, it might be if the sellers are in a "one and done" transactional sales environment. All of us have certainly seen salespeople with high degrees of drive but low empathy. They can be effective. But I'd argue that even in a quick sale, they might tend to overpower customers. And if the sales cycle is longer and you have a long-term relationship with a customer, sellers who only have strong drive won't build any connection to their clients.

The attribute of drive on psychotherapist Rick Breden's Behavioral Essentials Success Survey is called "proactivity." And, like Peter McCampbell, Breden would tell you it is critical to sales success. His Behavioral Essentials Success Survey measures twenty-one different behavioral attributes. On their assessment, aggression joins proactivity as a critical sales skill. Aggression, in this context, has to do with competitiveness along with a sense of urgency. Breden is quick to point out that when a salesperson has proactivity and aggression and also scores highly on what they call the "heart scales" of support and mentoring, that's when you can see magic. When a salesperson has a strong desire to win and the proactivity to make the calls, they are well on the way to sales success. But when that seller adds the attributes of Servant Heart Sellers we've outlined in this book, the level of success (and professional joy) skyrockets. Every seller interviewed for this book is loaded with drive. They want to win, and they like to win. But there is a fundamental difference. They believe that a true win is one where their client wins as well. They have found a way to channel their drive in a way that serves two masters: the desire to win and the desire to serve.

Full disclosure: I have used and believe in both the PXT Select and the Behavioral Essentials test. Rick Breden and Peter McCampbell are both friends and mentors of mine. Over the years, both have coached me through some challenging people issues. I recommend their work to anyone selecting salespeople. Both are Servant Heart Sellers themselves.

The Numbers Confirm What We Have Been Saying

Two weeks after I interviewed Rick Breden for this book, he suggested we do something to confirm the ideas we had discussed. He offered to have all the people interviewed for this book take the Behavioral Essentials evaluation. That way, we could see if the data about these amazing sellers gave us any confirmation of the principles in this book.

It was dramatic.

Like similar instruments, Breden's test measures a person's strengths and weaknesses with twenty-one different behavioral attributes. Several are critical for sales success. Obviously, pro-activity, which is the attribute that leads to a strong work ethic, has to be strong. So there is no surprise that our group of stars were high in that.

But there was a big contrast between our group and other salespeople. It was in the attribute called "support." Breden's test measure people on a scale of 1-100. He says he typically sees salespeople testing in the thirties in the support attribute. That's especially true in what he calls the "always be closing," old-school selling personality. Our Servant Heart Sellers group? They all tested above forty, most *way* above that. When Breden describes what this attribute means, it was almost like he had already read this book: "A lot goes into this scale. I think of ideas like emotional intelligence. I think of nurturing, and I think of deep caring."

To Breden, it's pretty clear that when you combine a high support score with the normal sales attributes, you have a recipe for a sales star. And the data proves it.

Here is one other data point you may find interesting: our group tested below the norm for salespeople in an attribute called "change." Breden says this suggests that they tend to want to stick with something and build something. And they also tend to have more traditional values like staying with a career. Breden says, "I just thought it was really interesting that the change scores were so low because I had not seen that pattern with salespeople typically."

This research came back after I had already written much of this book. I had already written Lesson Two: Play the Long game. The data about change is obviously very consistent with a group of salespeople committed to building something for the long term.

This research suggests that, going forward, we will be able to predict who is likely to be a Servant Heart Seller, a project we'll surely be working on in the next few years.

❧ PART 3 ❧

WHEN THE GOING GETS TOUGH

How do Servant Heart Sellers perform in challenging times?

For many salespeople, the year of the COVID-19 pandemic
was a time of incredible difficulty. I've sold during five reces-
sions and one global financial crisis. I've seen rough times. But
for many industries, this one might have won the prize for
the most challenging. It is challenging because, in addition to
business conditions, it's also totally changed the way we sell. I
recently was asked what my biggest surprise was in 2020. The
answer was easy. It's the amount of sales our JDA team was closing for our TV station clients....on Zoom. As someone who had
an entire career selling and teaching face-to-face selling, that
pivot—from both buyers and sellers—was amazing to watch.
And I am guessing that way of selling will become part of our
"new normal."

Some of the people profiled in this book went through a few months in 2020 that were horrible. Advertising sellers were especially hard hit. Most major TV groups reported 40–50 percent declines in core revenue in the second quarter of 2020. That's a big hit for salespeople. There were supply chain issues as well. Meg Linne from PepsiCo shared that aluminum shortages significantly impacted beverage manufacturer's ability to give their grocery chain customers all the soda and beer they wanted. With everyone drinking way more soda (and beer!) at home, that made sense, of course. But who knew that global supply chain would be an issue that would impact salespeople? But that's happening to a lot of sellers in the aftermath of the COVID-19 pandemic shutdowns.

But here's what we know: there are always opportunities in challenging times. And Servant Heart Sellers generally prospered during the COVID-19 pandemic. And if prosperity didn't happen immediately because of business conditions, they planted seeds and deepened the relationships that will allow them to grow market share as times improve.

Market share is a concept that most sellers don't spend a lot of time thinking about. Market share is simply the percentage of the business in a segment that your company does compared to its competition. Here's an example: If one thousand Fords were sold this month in your town, and Dealer A sold two hundred, then they have a 20 percent market share. Smart businesses are always trying to determine market share because it's a great indicator of the success of a company's marketing efforts. When market share is growing, it's generally an indication that a company is doing more things right than wrong. Conversely, when market share is declining, businesses should get nervous, because that suggests something might not be right.

When is the easiest time to grow market share? It's in a challenging market. In good times, everyone is able to be more aggressive in going out after business. It's pretty common that market leaders actually lose market share in a robust market. But when things get tough, that creates extraordinary opportunity.

I asked Mattress Mac about this when I interviewed him for this book in July 2020. Gallery Furniture dominates the Houston furniture market. They are considered one of the most successful furniture chains in America. I shared a stage with Mac years ago when we both spoke at the same conference. By then, I already knew that they had the highest sales per square foot of any furniture store in America. How did Gallery Furniture do during the pandemic? You guessed it. Jim McIngvale (Mattress Mac) confirmed that, just like in other challenging times, their business was doing great. And he jokingly added, "I'm really good at chaos."

Turns out Servant Heart Sellers are pretty good at chaos also. Or to say it differently, it's easier for them to seize the opportunities that a challenging environment gives them than it is for competitors. When I reached out to them about their experiences during 2020, they had a lot of stories of success.

It's pretty easy to see why that would occur. Remember Don Beveridge's point about peddlers versus partners? So many sales reps are seen as peddlers by their customers. They sell "stuff." But Servant Heart Sellers form true, long-term partnerships with their customers. Shamire Goodwin shared the story of one of his clients about whom he said, "If you asked her if I was her partner, she'd say, 'No, he's like my son.'" That sounds like a pretty close relationship to me!

Servant Heart Sellers build tons and tons of trust, because over time, the customer sees their huge desire to make a difference. Trust is huge. When you trust someone, you will share your secrets with them and your deepest fears. And that means the seller who is a trusted partner can really help the customer sort out options. Oscar Mejia describes it well: "Definitely, the COVID-19 pandemic has been the most challenging time in my career. On the positive side, it has also shown me the value of building relationships with my clients, because throughout the toughest months of the pandemic, not only did we maintain a consistent communication, they relied on me for guidance and recommendations. No doubt relationships paid off because they also helped me generate referrals for brand-new business."

Think about the lessons we shared in this book: playing the long game, acute listening, doing what's right for the customer, and so many more. Contrast them to the vast majority of sellers who are doing just the opposite. In normal times, these lessons are why Servant Heart Sellers win. But in challenging times, the sellers we have profiled become sounding boards and trusted advisors. That creates some short-term opportunities for sure. But what it really does is set up an even deeper long-term relationship going forward.

And sometimes the rewards can be immediate and significant. For Dean Thibault's commercial bankers at Landmark Bank, the pandemic created opportunity. When the government put out their Payroll Protection Plan many of the bigger banks were slow to get information to their clients. But Landmark's team went into overdrive, not just to serve their existing relationships, but target other businesses that were not being served well by their current bank. Dean wrote me this a few months later:

> We also added many, many businesses we wanted to have bank with us. I can't begin to explain the gratitude we received from all these businesses, clients and prospects alike! The relationship with our clients was reinforced to the point they will be with us forever! The bonus is that many prospects were equally impressed by our communication and thoughtfulness. Our efforts were rewarded by many businesses that were not clients who took us up on our offer to help and subsequently moved their business to us. The passive effort of a number of banks resulted in the loss of several of their best clients.

You get new customers, and your competition loses them? That's called growing market share.

In case you missed it, there is another lesson in Landmark's approach to challenging times. They got on offense. They weren't passive. Servant's Heart Sellers are just as driven as any other type of salespeople. That's a given. They may have a very different approach to clients, but they want to win just as much (or more) than anyone. Where other people see challenge, they see opportunity. One of my smart teachers is car dealer Mark Boniol. Mark captured that attitude perfectly when he described turning around a Louisiana Ford dealership during a steep market decline: "Customers are buying something from somebody. It's my job to make sure it's from us." Like Mark, Landmark Bank saw a tremendous opportunity in challenging times. Gallery Furniture operates that way as well. And they win big. It's the combination of a way to sell that builds trust and a focused desire to win that combines for significant results.

And here's the bullet point you should take away: these companies and sellers do play a *long* game. They understand that if they grow market share in a challenging market, they'll get a huge win when the market starts to expand again because then they have a bigger share of a bigger market. And that's when it gets fun.

If you think your business was challenged during the COVID-19 pandemic, try selling tickets and luxury suites for a major league sports team. During 2020, Justin Gurney was overseeing sales of those products for the New Jersey Devils, a National Hockey League team. How tough were things for sports teams? Ten months into the COVID-19 pandemic, they still weren't sure when they would start playing games again or when their building, The Prudential Center, was going to re-open. It's pretty tough to be a salesperson for a business that is essentially shut down.

Most major league sports teams furloughed the salespeople who sell ticket programs. But the owner of the Devils, Harris Blitzer Sports and Entertainment, did not. Harris Blitzer, who also owns the Philadelphia 76ers in the NBA, kept their sales team intact. And they are continued to interact with customers. Talk about taking the long view!

So what were Justin Gurney's team members doing those months? Having in-depth conversations with their clients about the business issues a company was facing and about how entertaining customers was going to look after the COVID-19 pandemic. Gurney says that the sales process changes when the seller has to say, "Look, I am a salesperson. But I've got nothing to sell you." What replaces it? Multiple interactions that are deeper and more honest and open. Gurney says it had maybe less to do with the sales process and more to do with simple humanity. The Devil's salespeople changed their relationships with many of their customers. An opportunity that came in a challenging time.

All major league sports teams struggled, make no mistake about that. But the teams who rely on what Gurney calls "the hustle metrics" likely hurt the most. Hustle metrics are a common measurement for many sales organizations. How many calls did you make? How many people did you ask to buy? Many sales leaders were taught by managers who did that and continued that approach when they got promoted. Managers pound their teams for activity—"If all you have is a hammer, everything is a nail." In a time of abundance, perhaps hustle metrics work. When the economy is booming, there is a case to be made that if you make enough calls, you can find buyers, almost by accident. But for major league sports teams, the COVID-19 year was the opposite of a time of abundance. There are few industries that were as challenged. Making a hundred calls a day is a recipe for disaster.

What will be the long-term win for the Devils? Gurney believes their pipeline is full of people they can engage with as major league hockey returns. He believes, and I agree, that the connections they have built will pay huge dividends for their revenue down the line. He's quick to acknowledge how wonderful it is to work for a company who has treated their people the way Harris Blitzer has. And he knows that's reducing sales turnover, which will also have a positive impact. He told me,

"Customers were actually leading us to discussing when we think games will begin again."

This revenue win for the Devils will be caused by a sales team that turns toward their customers at a time when most everyone else in their space is turning away, even furloughing the people that customers used to deal with. The New York/New Jersey metropolitan area has tons of sports teams. Would you like to bet on who's going to come out of the blocks on fire when the sports business gets back to normal? I'll take the Devils and give you points

Challenging times are times of huge opportunity for sellers and companies that are committed to their customers. Our Servant's Heart Sellers forge deeper relationships with clients than most. These relationships have a foundation of trust. If I run a company that is trying to figure out how to navigate through a tough time, who do I rely on for advice and counsel? It's the people I trust. The people interviewed for this book build those kinds of relationships. That always serves them well. But it makes an even bigger impact in a challenging market.

What does a challenging environment mean for Servant's Heart Sellers? Opportunity.

MANAGING SERVANT
HEART SELLERS

Do you feel lucky to have some Servant Heart Sellers on your team? Or is it an absolute pain?

Or is it a little bit of both, depending on the hour or the day?

The good news is that the more Servant Heart sellers you have, the more likely you are to meet your sales goals. And you'll know that the customers they work with will likely be with you for a long time.

You'll sometimes need to remember that. Because the bad news is Servant Heart Sellers can often be extremely challenging to manage. Your feelings about them can sometimes be love and sometimes be hate, often in the same day.

There are two things you need to always remember if you lead Servant Heart Sellers. The first is that they will cause more internal problems simply because they sell more. I once had a support person ask me why our top salesperson caused so many issues. His thinking is that if this seller went away, his life would be so much easier. But I am thinking I wish I had five more just like the rep who was his problem child.

High-volume salespeople always require more of a leader's time. More support, more customer issues, and occasionally more nudges and intervention. I've seen too many managers forget that stars require more because stars sell more!

And Servant Heart Sellers create another issue for managers. They can be so customer-oriented that at times, managers can wonder if the salesperson forgets who they work for. Listen to Oscar Mejia describe how he sees his role: "Everybody's important in a company, but my reputation is more important in front of my clients than the whole company because I'm the one on the line with my customers, and they have to have this trust with me."

There can be tension between managers and Servant Heart Sellers. Many can be very stubborn about taking something to a client they don't personally believe in. They sometimes don't care much about how important a new product is to you or your company. If they don't think it makes sense for their client, you can be pretty sure they won't present it.

In his role with our training and consulting company, JDA.media's Jim Stoos works with sellers all over America. He sees this customer focus with top sellers all the time. According to Stoos, "The top Servant Heart Sellers don't calculate commissions generally, so they're more concerned about the relationship than the sale. It would be out of character for them to slam a product in front of a client that they don't think is what the client needs. They just generally won't do that."

What's a manager to do? You need to understand something

very clearly. Servant Heart Sellers won't feel good about selling something they don't personally believe in. If you are their boss, you need to always be aware of that and then realize that if you want them to sell something, your job is to sell them. I've long thought that one of the biggest jobs sales managers have is to sell (and often resell) the sales team on the company's products. That sales effort is even more important with your Servant Heart Sellers. Managers have to sell them so they can feel good about selling their customers. Ask them directly how they really feel. That's hard to do. But with strong, confident people like we've profiled in this book, you can be sure they have an opinion. Don't mistake silence for agreement.

Once Servant Heart Sellers get comfortable with what the product can do for their clients, they'll present it with enthusiasm. But until that happens, they are going to be skeptics. And they may even influence others on your team because these sellers are perceived as leaders by their colleagues.

Servant Heart Sellers will be advocates for their clients with their bosses and with others inside the company they work for. Remember that they are totally committed to their customers and even more committed to the outcomes the customer is paying for. Because they are great communicators, they can be persuasive. Because they are great salespeople, they are used to winning their arguments. That can frequently cause tension between Servant Heart Sellers and their bosses. Rhonda Kuhlman shared, "My managers will actually tell my clients this: 'Rhonda comes in and argues with us about things on your behalf.' It's true. I'm not afraid of a good, healthy professional argument."

But how do managers handle those disagreements? It's a

huge mistake to play the authority card. "Because I said so" is a comment that doesn't resonate with any employee very well. But it has even more negative impact with these stars. Want to drive a Servant Heart Seller away? Act like you don't care about their customer outcomes. They will find it very tough to work for bosses who don't support their commitment to customers.

What does work? Acute listening combined with fairness and transparent communication. Yes, you will occasionally need to remind them who they work for. But you also better be listening to their advocacy on behalf of their clients. And your sellers need to know you are listening.

A great leader once told me that he was very clear with his top sellers. He said, "Don't judge me by any single decision I make. Because, for sure, you won't like some of them. Judge me by all the decisions I make. And then tell me if you think I have been fair. If you don't think I have been fair, I want to know about it."

One of the current cliché leadership words right now is "transparency." Transparency with a top seller about your need to balance their desire to serve their clients with your need to protect the best interest of the company is essential. Also essential is making sure that even in the middle of your professional disagreements, your star sellers know how grateful you are that they work for your company. Honoring your stars and acknowledging the impact they have creates a climate that helps you deal with uncomfortable issues.

It is about whether these sellers can trust their managers. Can your Servant Heart Seller trust that you will hear them out and not reject their concerns instantly? Can they trust that you also have a strong desire to serve customers? Do they trust that you are a person of absolute integrity?

Great leaders create a culture of trust. And that becomes the foundation of all the conversations you'll have with your team members.

Leading a Servant Heart Seller? Here's a recap of what you need to remember:

- Stars create more problems because stars sell more stuff.

- Servant Heart Sellers need to be sold themselves on any new product or initiative before they'll sell their customers. That's a sale you must make as their manager.

- Don't mistake silence for agreement. Ask them directly how they feel.

- Make sure every conversation with them demonstrates your recognition of the contribution they make to the team. You'll need to listen, listen, and then listen some more to their advocacy for their clients. Listen before you respond.

And while it's necessary to occasionally remind folks who their paychecks come from, be careful. Very careful. Servant Heart Sellers aren't going to be comfortable working for a company that rejects their values. And you want to do all you can to keep these folks on your team, no matter how many challenges they will give you.

Did I mention listening? Respectful listening?

Managing Servant Heart Sellers requires maturity. Managers have to balance the incredible impact that a star brings a company with the frequent tension they will create. These sellers won't always be easy to manage. But the rewards from having these people on your team are great. Finding that balance is so worthwhile for you and your company.

CREATING A SERVANT HEART SELLING CULTURE: BUILDING THE TEAM

WHEN A SHIP MISSES THE HARBOR, IT IS RARELY THE HARBOR'S FAULT. —NEIL DEMPSTER, PhD, MBA, CLEARVIEW PERFORMANCE SYSTEMS

WHAT KIND OF IMPACT COULD YOUR COMPANY HAVE IN YOUR MARKET IF YOUR ENTIRE SALES EFFORT WAS ORGANIZED AROUND THE IDEA OF SERVANT HEART SELLING? How would that look? How would your customers compare you with your competition? Would that positively impact your profitability?

If you're a boss or company leader reading this book, I am betting you get it. This is a way to sell that can increase revenues, profitability, and loyalty. Is it tough to create an entire team of

Servant Heart Sellers? The answer is *yes*. But it is being done. And when it happens, the impact can be significant.

One of my early business teachers was a smart car dealer named Mark Boniol. Mark has always impressed me. When I first met him, he was operating a Ford store in Shreveport, Louisiana. He had dramatically increased sales and market share for a Ford dealer despite the market being challenged by a long period of low oil prices, a regional recession for Texas and Louisiana.

Because I was an advertising person, I wanted Mark to ascribe his success to brilliant marketing. But he was quick to correct my thinking. He believed that three ingredients had to be in place before any marketing efforts had a chance to be successful.

In Mark's view, successful businesses needed the following:

1. People

2. Process

3. Systems and controls

The business leaders I interviewed for this book would likely agree with Mark. They are building businesses around those three pillars to create highly successful companies with strong commitments to customers. This chapter is about the lessons we can learn by looking at the companies they have created.

If You Don't Know Where You're Going, Any Road Will Get You There!

Before starting to work on Mark Boniol's three pillars, leaders must be committed themselves. Do the values in this book represent the company that you want to lead? Are you prepared—really prepared—that there might be short-term consequences to getting your company aligned with these principles? How about your bosses or partners? Are they on board? This is a big deal. There is so much focus on short-term results for business owners today that many companies are not comfortable making that kind of commitment to how long it takes to really change a culture. And some simply don't want to take the possible hit to profits. And that might especially be the case for publicly-traded companies that are very focused on their quarterly reporting and stock price. Frankly, I think those fears are usually not real. But leaving behind some of the transactional, "we need to make the quarter" practices can be frightening or resisted by your bosses.

Remember the second lesson from Servant Heart Sellers in this book? It's about taking the long view. That is also a big deal for leaders. Leaders must have a personal vision and the guts to believe in it as they create the organization that serves that vision.

Much is written about leadership because it's so important. This is not a leadership book, but I will say this: it's never the passengers who crash the plane. You'll never see a headline that reads, "Plane Crash in Sarasota. Passenger Error." Pilots crash planes. The famous line about a fish rotting from the head down? The opposite is also true. Culture starts with the leader. When leadership has a vision (and the guts to move in that direction), that is the foundation for inspiring people to change and align with that vision.

I have worked with hundreds of sales staff over the last thirty years. And I can tell you with absolute certainty that the difference between high-performing groups and the teams that are average has little to do with the team. Almost every sales team has a couple of stars, a few who are decent, and a couple who should be considering other career opportunities. It's the leaders who make the difference. That cannot be emphasized enough.

The VanDevere family owns car dealerships in Akron, Ohio, including a Chevy and Kia store. Mike VanDevere is clear about their vision. He described a process that I see a lot: "We created our culture. I would say it evolved. I would say we've lived it. Then, we really put it on paper and displayed and communicated with every applicant. We've done that for the last ten or twelve years. Prior to that, it was not in as much detail as it is today."

As Mike's company expanded, he felt they needed to formally put their beliefs on paper. He says, "When I came to work here, we had forty-three employees. We have about three hundred fifty now. To me, I think the bigger you get, the more you have to spell things out and lay it out and have a leadership team that also buys into your culture."

The VanDevere culture draws from their roots as a family-owned business. They even use the word "family" to set out the framework of their culture.

F = Faith
A = Attitude
M = Motivation
I = Integrity
L = Love
Y = Yahoo, Yippee ("celebrate")

Spend an hour with Mike, as I did before writing this book, and you'll realize how important these attributes are to him. Mike doesn't have any requirement that his team members share his faith. But they want people to know that it is a foundational principle. When he spoke of the word "attitude," he immediately said, "Not just at work." Even in a quick conversation, you get the sense that Mike genuinely cares about his team members as people. It's not just about how they perform when they are at the dealerships.

How does Mike's family culture impact his business? You can be certain VanDevere will attract people who share his values. Customers get treated incredibly well because the team is treated incredibly well. His repeat business and customer loyalty numbers are very, very strong. And that drives the bottom line. But Mike's clear that profit isn't his biggest goal. Taking care of his people and taking care of his customers is what drives him.

He says, "Every year, we set aside eight weeks where I buy everybody lunch once a week, and we go through some form of training or book about things that are more about life than just about my business." Mike cares about his people as people. And they know it.

You may be thinking that it's easier to demonstrate that kind of caring when you are a family-owned company or don't have a lot of debt. And that may be true. I've been an overleveraged entrepreneur at different points in my life. Much of that time, I wasn't always doing a lot of long-term thinking. It's hard to be a long-term thinker when you are checking the mail to see if enough money came in today! Been there, done that, and had to sell the T-shirt to pay the electric bill!

But Mark Boniol changed his culture in a challenging time. And Dean Thibault's Landmark National Bank does it as a publicly traded company (Nasdaq: LARK). Dean has a clear vision of what commercial banking looks like at Landmark. But simply deciding that they wanted their people to be bankers, not lenders, isn't enough. They have to provide the training and tools to make that a reality. Dean does have a vision. It's a vision that says they are going to offer real value to their business clients. That's way more than just selling loans.

Leaders lead. But first they have to pick the road they are heading down. That's why establishing the vision for your organization is huge.

THEY STUDY WHAT YOU DO ... NOT WHAT YOU SAY

IF YOU WANT PEOPLE TO BE IN THE OFFICE BY 8:00 A.M.,
YOU NEED TO BE HERE AT 7:30 A.M. THEY STUDY WHAT YOU
DO, NOT WHAT YOU SAY.
—RON FRIZZELL (MY SECOND BOSS) TO A YOUNG MAN-
AGER NAMED JIM DOYLE

PERHAPS YOU CAN IMAGINE THE SCENE. It's your first sales meeting after being back from a big training conference or a corporate meeting. You announce some change in procedure because of what you learned while you were away. The new salespeople on your team are nervous. But they are reassured by your veterans, who assure them, saying, "Don't worry, he gets over it. He always does." That may not be the way your sales team reacted, but it surely was what happened for much of my time as a sales leader. My team could tell you that I was very good at starting things. I can easily get excited about a great idea. But I was pretty weak at finishing. My enthusiasm for new ideas was greater than my accountability and follow-through.

One of the biggest lessons I had to learn as a young manager trying to become an effective manager was this: Start less things. But be sure the things you start get finished. One of the biggest lessons I have learned from working with sales managers for the last thirty years is that it is the absolute commitment of leadership that determines whether any idea lasts for a moment or becomes a long-term part of the culture.

That starts with retaining and recruiting great people. That's huge. But that isn't close to being enough unless you have the systems and controls in place to turn great people into a long-term culture. As a trainer, I am used to seeing client bosses give passionate speeches at the end of my training sessions. They'll talk about how the material I've presented is going to be their new operating system. That would be incredibly gratifying if I didn't know that, in most cases, their commitment will diminish quickly, usually within the next few weeks and months: "Don't worry, he gets over it. He always does."

The Servant Leader

The term "servant leadership" began as an essay written by Robert H. Greenleaf in 1970. According to the Center for Servant Leadership, the organization that continues Greenleaf's legacy work, "A servant-leader focuses primarily on the growth and well-being of people and the communities to which they belong. While traditional leadership generally involves the accumulation and exercise of power by one at the top of the pyramid, servant leadership is different. The servant-leader shares power, puts the needs of others first, and helps people develop and perform as highly as possible."

Greenleaf never claimed he was a servant leader, but that was his aspiration. And if you are going to build a sales organization that is loaded with Servant Heart Sellers, it's likely that should be what you aspire to as well. Servant leaders are generally humble. They usually believe they'll never actually achieve that vision. But they work to become more consistent at leading in a way that is in sync with servant leadership principles.

Psychologist Rick Breden's company, Behavioral Essentials, has tested thousands of leaders. In their test, they look for a number of attributes. Successful leaders are proactive. They have a need to be in charge. A biggie is endurance, which is the attribute of finishing what you start. That is also critical. But Breden adds one thing that distinguishes long-term successful leaders. It's measured in his test's support scale. Breden says this: "Over the years of doing leadership and leadership studies and testing so many leaders, I've found that when it comes to holding a team together, it's almost impossible to do that if you don't have some kind of a Servant Heart." Breden believes that the support scale is critically important to building successful organizations.

I am guessing that if you have gotten to this point in this book, you are already inclined to lead this way. Many leaders have many of the servant leader attributes long before they declare themselves to be servant leaders. If your heart is already there, then the goal is to become more consistent at leading in this way. The podcasts and resources of the Center for Servant

Leadership (greenleaf.org) are great resources for you if you want to formalize that journey.

What Is Your Sales Process?

As car dealer Mark Boniol taught me, having a vision and a heart for service isn't enough. You must have a sales process that is consistent.

What does that look like? This will differ by industry. RXBAR's Jasmine Ruschmann offers a full nutrition bar category overview to a new buyer. Landmark National Bank's team starts with an in-depth diagnosis following a fairly specific script that is designed to discover if there's a customer need that the bank might help with. As a leader, it's relatively easy to figure out what a Servant Heart Selling process looks like for your industry. Just look at the ten lessons that the Servant Heart Sellers taught us that are outlined in this book. Then ask yourself what the most significant lessons that you should make sure are part of your process are.

One key point for you to consider is this: of all the lessons our Servant Heart Sellers shared, the one that is most often ignored is about the importance of asking lots of good questions. Sadly, most sellers don't ask anywhere near enough questions. They are so driven to sell that they shortchange the diagnosis process to more quickly move to their agenda. And, yes, this includes your sales team, no matter how good you think they are. My personal proof of that statement? For several years, I'd done a training where we'd split the sellers into groups of four or five to do a roleplay for a fictitious new client. All these teams have been my training sessions where I have stressed and stressed the need for diagnosis. They've made diagnosis calls with our consultant team where questioning is the base. So take a guess about how long it is until someone asks a question about the specifics of their advertising investments. Ninety percent of the time, that's happening in the first two minutes. That's not really a true diagnosis call. They may be asking questions, but the questions aren't about the customer's real issues. They are more about the seller's agenda to make a sale. The seller is asking questions, so they may think they are doing diagnosis. But in reality, they aren't even close.

As I reflect on the ten lessons from our Servant Heart sellers, I also think playing the long game is something that most could improve. When Steve Litwer was running ad sales for Mediacom, he built a formal aftercare program that included making commitments for extensive follow-up with customers *after* the sale. As a leader, he wanted his sellers to build relationships for the long term. And as you can imagine, the sellers who were the most diligent in following that formal program also had the lowest churn.

Much of the Mediacom program was designed to make the seller a resource to their customers. They used that process to differentiate themselves from the myriad of advertising choices that a local business owner could choose. Playing the long game and being very different from the competition is important for all of us today.

Just Say No!

The customer is not always right. And Servant Heart Sellers push back when they feel a customer is making a mistake. They say *no* when most sellers would say *yes*. More than a few managers also make that mistake. I know. One of my common mistakes as an entrepreneur was taking deals that really weren't right for us or for the customer. And why would I do that? Fear, sometimes driven by a challenging year or uneven marketplace. I've learned the hard way that those are almost always the situations that either don't turn out well or consume huge amounts of leadership time, often well out of proportion to the amount of business they represent.

Remember, your team is studying what you do, not what you say. So if I preach Servant Heart Selling as a leader but I continue to take transactional deals just to get the money in the door, what is the real message that is sent to my team?

System, Not Seminar

A sales process can be introduced in a training session or seminar. But to make them *your* culture, the ideas and techniques must be repeated and repeated and coached and coached. And then repeated and coached again.

Advertising people study how messages get ingrained in people's heads. That concept is called "frequency." Frequency is defined as the number of times an ad reaches someone who is a potential customer. We used to teach ad people that the magic number was three, that an ad should reach a consumer three times. But today's consumers and the people on your sales teams are the most bombarded group in history. It's not just the number of ads. Think about the number of emails, texts, and other information that makes this the most cluttered communication time in the history of the world. So if you only expose an ad or your training on great diagnosis calls to your team only three times, you are likely being lost in the clutter. Today, we coach businesses to look at frequency numbers way higher than that to achieve real impact.

So what does that mean to you as a sales manager? If the training about some part of your sales process has just a one-time-only exposure, you'll never really turn that training into a system. It will never become your culture without high repetition of the elements that are essential to your success.

As a manager, you are probably thinking that people would be sick of hearing the message even before the third time. And you'd be sick of delivering it, right? Please know this: it takes a lot longer than you think to ingrain key sales processes into your culture. And you can lose them quickly if they aren't repeated over and over again.

A Quick Word about Training

I have made my living as a sales trainer. So you might be surprised I would say this. You will never train your way to excellence. Training without follow-up becomes an event. It's what happens *after* the training that determines if this becomes a system or just another seminar. One idea for great leaders: keep any positive training experience alive by having team members do a quick ten-minute summary, one each week, of one part of a training experience. That keeps it alive. And we know that if you really want to learn something, go teach it. Doing that has the benefit of getting each of your sellers more comfortable with the concepts they are teaching. And it's the same message, but not repeated by you. In our experience at JDA, that simple decision indicates whether a new client of ours will truly take the content we've presented and make it a long-term part of their process.

What Do You Applaud?

Different personality styles prefer to be communicated with in different ways. I have learned so much from the lessons about communication styles in Wilson Learning Social Styles program or Tony Alessandra's Platinum Rule.

These programs use assessments to determine someone's communication style. They are great training for sellers as it shows them how to modify their approach based on the preferred style of their customer.

This training helped me as a seller, but it had the most impact when I was a sales leader. I learned that 70 percent of most sales teams test as Expressives (Social Styles) or Socializers (Platinum Rule) on a four-quadrant scale. Each quadrant has their primary motivations. Drivers/Directors want results. Amiables/Relaters want harmony. Analyticals/Thinkers want accuracy and order. What about Socializers/Expressives? Their key motivations are excitement, fun, and *applause*.

A common management axiom is that we don't get what we expect; we get what we inspect. And maybe that's true. But for sales leaders, it might be even more true that we get what we applaud, especially for the 70 percent in the Expressive/Socializer quadrant. They *love* applause (and fun!). Let's suppose that one of the foundational pieces of your Servant Heart Selling Culture is to do really deep-dive diagnosis. Try really ingraining that in your culture by publicly applauding any time a salesperson does a great job with a diagnosis call. I guarantee you that the behavior you applaud will get repeated because most who are Socializers crave positive recognition.

As a manager, I always applauded the sale. There's absolutely nothing wrong with that. But make sure you don't just applaud what comes out of the bottom of your sales funnel. Applaud the actions that help you build the culture you envision. And you will see that behavior becomes more consistent in your sales process.

How Do You Keep from Drifting Away?

The great trainer Don Beveridge used to say something that always resonated with me. He'd talk about the difference between D/K and D/E. D/K stood for a deficiency of knowledge, and D/E stood for a deficiency of execution. Beveridge believed that that challenge for most organizations wasn't a deficiency of knowledge. People know what to do. The issues were always in execution. All I can say to that is *amen*.

It's easy to begin the new shiny idea or adapt a selling philosophy like the one we've outlined in this book. The real challenge is the tough slog that it takes to turn the ideas into culture. Consultants make a lot of money introducing the new shiny idea.

But it will only be the leaders who determine whether that idea becomes the selling culture of their company, a culture that can lead to long-term success.

I have such admiration for leaders like Landmark National Bank's Dean Thibault who can do that. Dean's teams don't have sales meetings. They call them progress meetings. They will role play first meetings with clients during these sessions. Most sellers hate role playing. But Landmark works to create an environment where trust is huge, and people don't have to be afraid of messing up in the practice session. After all, it's better to mess up in practice than in the actual game. After the call, the banker of Dean's team will be debriefed. How did it go? What did you say that was effective? Did you have any awkward moments you can learn from? What worked? What are next steps?

That's a powerful exercise from a training perspective. It will help the banker be more prepared. But I'd suggest to you the real value is that that process communicates to the entire team over and over again that this is our sales process. And that might be the real value.

Execution trumps ideas. I don't write that to put down ideas. I love great ideas that make us better. But having worked with sales teams for thirty years, I can say with absolute certainty that execution is way more important than good ideas. The leaders who execute are the ones who truly achieve change.

Engaged Leadership

Some people are fans of musicians or movie stars. The people I admire run sales departments or businesses. And I am a huge fan of Patrick Caudill. Patrick is one of the partners in Gold Rush BBQ in Venice, Florida, just south of Sarasota.

I had eaten at Gold Rush occasionally over the years. But I really got to study it as a business during a time when both of my children worked there. Before he went to college, my son, Brian, worked there as a bus boy. Later, my daughter, Cassie, worked at the to-go order pickup window.

A few years after he had worked there, Brian was home from college and wanted to go to Gold Rush for dinner. Brian's close friend, another former Gold Rush busboy, was with us. So our table had two former employees, plus my daughter, who still worked there. And once again, I had a chance to watch Patrick run his business close up.

The next morning, I was thinking about what I saw, and the word that came to me was "engaged." Patrick is engaged in every part of his business.

He is highly engaged with his employees. He really knew those kids, asked about their girlfriends, joked with them, and talked sports with the boys. It was clear he liked them. It was clear they really liked him. Brian told me that while busing tables wasn't "fun," Patrick kept the atmosphere upbeat. With the exception of these college-bound kids whom they knew would leave at some point, the Gold Rush turnover is probably as low as I have ever seen in a restaurant.

Patrick is also engaged with his customers, saying hi to the regulars, checking in to see how the food is. (And it's always great!) Brian used to work in another restaurant in Sarasota. He said that owner never really spent any time in the restaurant. He was always out back, far away from the customers. You can't be distant from your customers in any business today, especially not in a restaurant.

Finally, Patrick is totally engaged with his business. Every time I have been there when the restaurant is busy, Patrick will be cleaning off tables, not looking around for one of the kids to do it. He does it himself. That increases his table turn and keeps customers from waiting too long. And it sets an incredible example to his team of action and urgency. He's a worker, not just a boss.

He pays attention to the little things as well. At one point on a Saturday evening, I saw him on the floor picking up a scrap of paper that had fallen beneath a table.

Engaged leadership. I think businesses today need a lot more Patricks!

You don't lead people by dictate.

You cannot inspire and excite your team by email.

You can't be a leader today and stay office bound.

It's not about pronouncing things at the sales meeting and then closing the door of your office. It's about being available—more than available as a coach, teacher, and cheerleader. It means sitting in the bull pen making appointment calls yourself if you are asking your team to do that.

Engaged leadership.

I think engaged means more than just being there. It's a deep involvement, a passion perhaps.

How engaged are you with your team? How would your team answer that? Are you talking to them all the time? Cheering their successes and commiserating with them about their challenges? Do they know you care about them and have their back?

Are you engaged—really engaged—with customers? I talk to way too many managers who have allowed the paperwork requirements of their jobs to keep them away from customers. They tell me they never get out of the office. That is horrible. Some leaders can't even find time to see customers when the customer is in their office for something else. That won't work today. We don't have a business without customers. I know you know that. But does the way you use your time reflect the importance of customers?

Are you engaged with the business? What is the equivalent of Patrick's personally busing the tables for you? The leaders interviewed for this book are in different industries. I'd consider all of them engaged leaders.

❧ PART 4 ❧

THE PATH TO TRUE JOY
AND SUCCESS

SALES IS HARD. Most people who have never been in sales have no idea how hard it is. Salespeople face rejection daily. I joke that a new salesperson today gets more rejection in their first year of sales than I got in my seventh-grade dance. (And that wasn't pretty.)

Sales is hard. There's the economic uncertainty of being paid based on commission. Some people call that being unemployed every Monday. That's because you can't ever stop developing business. Salespeople know there is only one way to coast . . .

and it's not uphill.

Sales is hard. Salespeople face additional pressure to make quota and additional scrutiny when they don't.

Sales is hard. Most salespeople live in fear of losing a large client. Those losses can come in completely random ways. One day, your relationship is solid. The next day, a new buyer or new corporate owner comes in, and your business relationship changes.

Sales is hard. Not every sales manager is great. And some managers take the pressure they are under and turn that on their sales team in ways that are neither productive or fun.

Sales is hard!

So why do we do it? Most great sellers would admit they love the competition. They enjoy persuading. And then there's the money. Salespeople are paid for results. So there is always the potential to give yourself a raise and make a lot of money. Many of us are C students making A money—or in my case, way lower than a C student.

Yes. Sales can be hard. But the people I got to know while researching this book love what they do. Really love it. Like Bill Gangloff said, "I'm not burned out at work. I mean, I've literally been doing the same thing in the same office for the same company for thirty-one years." And if you spent time on Zoom with Bill, you'd see that his energy, commitment to clients, and joy with his work was front and center.

Much research that suggests that serving others helps us find more joy. But those discussions often talk about doing that through volunteering or doing little things for someone else. Even little things like returning the grocery cart can bring us a spark of joy.

I am pretty sure Servant Heart Sellers do all those things. But they have also found that there's a path to increased joy and happiness in their work. AJ Vaden was pretty direct about that. She said, "As I made my transition from being a transactional seller to a more consultative sale, my joy level went up."

AJ and so many other salespeople have consciously decided to make their work about serving others. As they do that, they discovered so much more joy from their work. When the focus becomes less on making a sale and more on making a difference, the joy level increases a lot.

Don't get me wrong—AJ loves to sell. She loves to close business. But it's incredibly important to her to sell a customer something that really makes a difference, and that small tweak in her motivation changes everything. And guess what? Not only will she have a lasting impact on her clients, but she'll also get real satisfaction from her work.

My first sales job five decades ago was in a car dealership. I only lasted about six months. The culture of that dealership was about as opposite of Mike VanDevere's dealership as a culture could possibly be. I clearly didn't understand the principles of this book at that point in my career, but I figured out something pretty quickly. One of the major roles of the salesperson at this dealership was to figure out how savvy the customer was so we could extract the highest gross profit possible from the deal. When people are talking about a customer and saying things like "I stuck it to him" (which is a way of saying the customer paid way too much), it didn't feel right. I remember being part of a deal for a big used truck that was the biggest gross profit deal of the year because the buyer was not sophisticated. I won't lie. I loved the commission. But I had a crappy feeling about the whole experience.

That kind of selling, and the sellers that practice it, defines winning as the primary goal. I win if I make a sale. And if it's a sale with a huge profit, that's even better. That kind of selling can feel like manipulation. And the people who practice it are likely the ones who want to study every closing technique, thinking they can somehow trick the customer into buying.

I am positive that stuff does not work. If all you are is focused on winning, how does that make your customers feel? But also think about how that makes you feel! If your mindset is to "conquer" someone, then every day in sales is as hard as the day before. It never gets easier!

But it does get easier for Servant Heart Sellers. Rory Vaden says,

> When you're a Servant Heart Seller, then your reputation grows and grows and grows, ultimately to where it's doing most of the work for you in advance of where you start to attract people into your life based upon trust and credibility. They don't come to you with any fear or resistance that you're going to somehow convince them into something that isn't good for them or manipulate them. Not only do they come with no defenses, they come open and receptive. They come saying, 'Based upon what I've heard, you are who I'm drawn to. Is there a way that this is a fit?'

Rory adds, "I'm shocked that more people don't understand that."

Money manager Randy Muscagni has built a practice based

on those principles. He says, "From a sales standpoint, you position yourself where you try to attract assets as opposed to going after assets. If you ever get to the point where you attract a business and you can live on the harvest and not be too greedy and survive and grow from there, I think that's a better place for me than to be making cold calls."

One of the things that was so clear to me from the interviews I did for this book was how much our Servant Heart Sellers genuinely enjoyed what they did. The Conference Board says 53 percent of Americans are dissatisfied about their jobs. That's not our group. They love what they do. That doesn't mean there aren't stressors or challenges. There surely are. That doesn't mean that things happen, like the challenges of bad economy that negatively impact them. They get challenges all the time. But day in and day out, they find genuine satisfaction and joy from the work they do.

As I Serve More, I Make More

When I think about the people I've met doing this book, the idea that your clients become your sales force is so apparent. Ninety percent of the expensive motor coaches Dave Wall sells each year are to repeat and referred customers. Jeff Wagner does about ten times the mortgage volume as the average top performers in that business, almost all from people his referral sources have sent him. Mike VanDevere's dealerships have a very high number of repeat customers. That probably allows him to spend less money on marketing, which has a great impact on the store's profitability.

Most Servant Heart Sellers have ongoing relationships with their customers. They are seldom "one and done" sellers. In fact, people who are drawn to sell this way are not likely to be attracted to transactional selling. It won't be satisfying to them no matter how much money they can make.

The logic for Servant Heart Sellers is so simple that one wonders why more people haven't figured it out.

You help a client seize an opportunity or solve a problem.

Your solution works so the client keeps working with you.

That creates base of business that keeps going every year.

You'll become one of your company's top sellers because each of you start from a higher base, and you keep following that process with consistency—not just an occasional effort but your everyday approach to your business.

I Want the Sale, but I Don't Need the Sale

If you are relatively new to sales, this idea may seem far-fetched. But Servant Heart Sellers actually get to a point where they want to make a sale, but they don't *need* to make a sale. They especially don't need to make a sale if it feels like they aren't doing the right thing for the customer.

I am sure there are some people who are like that naturally. But I also think that for many of us, that is something we grow into as we get comfortable with this approach to customers. It also helps to have found some success that reduces the day-to-day financial pressure to sell something. Bill Gangloff sees that in his industry. He says, "I see how some folks live paycheck to paycheck. That desperation comes through. Obviously, to be successful long term, you can't be desperate. Moving beyond the need to make a sale is significant."

The people interviewed for this book often had some inclination to sell the way this book encourages from early on in their career. But making a full commitment to it sometimes came slower. So many are like Jasmine Ruschmann, who describes her personal path. Jasmine said, "I think I'm not necessarily intuitively that way in a business sense." Jasmine told us she was a *D* on the DISC profile. That's the Driver. She shared that when she first got into sales, "It wasn't that I didn't care about that stuff, but I was always like, 'Okay, we've got to get this done.' Or 'I need to solve whatever problem we're going through for the customer.'"

Jasmine learned over time that she had to make the same type of connection with her customers that she made in her personal life. As she says, "That took experience and learning how to make a connection."

Servant Heart Sellers aren't always born that way. Most have some natural instincts to serve, and with time and experience they get more committed to this selling path. They see results. And that causes them to become even more committed. So success creates more success. And it keeps growing.

Trust your instincts to serve. And trust that will create success for you.

My Personal Lessons

I am intensely driven to succeed.

That drive has served me well. But it's also created challenges as well, mostly with important relationships in my life. An early sales profile described me as being intensely driven and having good empathy skills "when I choose to use them." But the evaluator quickly added that "you won't always choose to use them." Sadly, my wife would likely agree.

Like most great salespeople, I serve two masters: the desire to win and the desire to make a difference. Here is an example: I wrote this book to serve a profession I love. That's the making a difference part. But I also want it to be successful.

Finding the balance between my two masters has caused problems over my career.

In the early days of my training business, I would end a seminar by making a big offer: "If I can ever help you with anything, please call me." And I meant it as I said it. But then I'd have a rare day in the office, and if you called, I'd go through the motions but not respond with the energy or concern I had promised. I am sure many times the person who called hung up, wondering where that great guy from the seminar had gone.

There were exceptions. If you were in a position to hire me again, I was very different! Then I would act like I had all the time in the world. I was never too busy for the bosses who had the ability to hire me again, only for the salespeople whom I had told to call me.

When you don't walk your talk, that's called being a hypocrite. And that's what I was doing.

It took me a while, but at some point, I came to understand exactly what was going on. I made a conscious decision to change. But I also began to articulate a new vision for our company. I began to see our business as a way to serve ... not a way to make money.

And you can probably guess what I am about to write. As I focused more on serving others and less on making money, you can guess what happened. Our business grew exponentially. Today, we are likely in the top 5 percent of all the speaking and training businesses in the United States. I am positive that happened in the aftermath of the decision to change our focus to serving.

Remember the Zig Ziglar line I quoted earlier: "You can have everything in life you want if you will just help other people get what they want."

In the late 1990s, two of my most powerful teachers and mentors, men who had never met each other, both suggested I read the same book. They did this within five days of each other. I think that's more than coincidental. So I bought the book. It was called *Love Is Letting Go of Fear* by Gerald Jampolsky. It's a book based on the lessons from a spiritual program called the *Course in Miracles.*

Talk about the student being ready and the teacher appearing! This book continues to be one of the five most impactful books in my life. For many years, I read it daily. Often, I spend an entire week studying just one of the lessons.

The first lesson in that book is the basis of this chapter. The title of that lesson? Everything I give is given to me in return.

Here's what I believe today: if I give love out to the world, I get love back. If I give away money, more money comes to me. But conversely, if I send out anger or frustration or sarcasm, guess what I get back?

The Buddhists call this karma. Jampolsky compares it with a boomerang, the idea that if I do good things, the universe will respond. This is way more than "what goes around comes around." This is a deep belief that I cause what comes into my life by the way I treat others and by what I put out into the world.

Here's just one example: a number of years ago, a client of mine got twisted up with his partners in a broadcast group. He basically got fired. Because I had gone through the same situation a few years earlier, I called him and invited him to Florida for a weekend. We talked about every emotion I had gone through when I had been fired by my partners, and I shared my story of that firing being a bridge to the life of joy the training business has brought to me. I had no agenda other than to help a guy I liked.

Fast-forward five years. We stayed in touch. He'd taken on some consulting work and looked at other deals. He called me one day and offered me a chance to invest in a new company he's started to acquire TV stations. That's something I thought I never would have had a chance to do. Ten years later, we sold the last of our stations. A significant portion of my wealth happened because of that friendship.

Everything you give is given in return.

More recently, a colleague and I were frustrated by an executive at a large client who did not agree with our view of the world. (Yes, that happens.) I kept telling my associate over and over, "He's not a bad guy. We just haven't sold him yet. But he's a great guy." In other words, we kept sending him love. The relationship turned around, and we now do lots of business with him.

I get examples of the power of this weekly, whether it's a

board meeting for a condo association, a big sales presentation, or the person who waits on me at the dry cleaner. Whatever I bring to them, I get back.

I have a choice in every single encounter I have today. Can I offer love and friendship? Or do I bring judgment or frustration? It's my belief that the way I answer that question in the way I treat others will determine so much of what happens in my life.

More Money, More Joy

This chapter began by talking about how hard selling can be. But it doesn't have to be that hard for you.

Servant Heart Sellers have found real joy in their work. They love what they do. Gallery Furniture's Jim McIngvale, aka Mattress Mac, has the energy of a thirty year old, and he's nearly seventy. He told me, "Work is life's greatest therapy." Mac is clear about why he works: "Because it's fun. What else would I do?"

I keep wishing you could have been on all the Zoom calls I did for this book. You would have met people with a true love for what they do. They sell different products and serve different industries. There are differences in the specifics of their sales processes. But they have all found a path to true joy.

And yes, they have achieved huge financial success.

More money and more joy? That sounds like a combination that is worth working toward.

THE POWER OF ACTION

GOD PROVIDES THE WIND. BUT MAN MUST RAISE THE
SAILS. —ST. AUGUSTINE

I HAVE ENDED ALMOST EVERY TRAINING SESSION THAT I'VE
DONE IN THE LAST THIRTY YEARS BY SAYING THIS: "TRAIN-
ING WITHOUT ACTION IS ENTERTAINMENT." We have a lot of
fun in our sessions. There's a lot of laughter. But the fact that we
had a good time doesn't mean we've had a productive session.
That will only be determined by the action we take *after* we leave
this place.

Action is critical. Action always trumps contemplation. It's
not what you learn but what you *do* with what you learn that will
determine your success.

So if the messages in this book have resonated with you,
now is the time to take action. You might start by reviewing the
principles of Servant Heart Selling as a way of taking inventory
about where you are in your career and how you may improve.

Most of us will have things we instinctively do pretty well and other areas we can improve. As you look at the list of things Servant Heart Sellers teach us, what can you do better?

Lesson One I Work for Them

Am I totally committed to customer outcomes?

Lesson Two Play the Long Game

Do I believe that if it's good for the client, it will ultimately be good for me? Do my actions support that belief?

Lesson Three Ask a Million Questions

How committed am I to asking questions to really determine client needs? How much time do I spend in diagnosis? Am I an acute listener?

Lesson Four Teach, Don't Sell

Do my sales presentations show the customer how the solution I offer can really help them? How effectively do I take away risk?

Lesson Five Closing Hard—The Quick Path to Failure

How do I get commitment without manipulative closing techniques? What does win-win selling look like in this area of my process?

Lesson Six It's Not about Relationships, It's about Trust

Do my customers truly trust me? Do they tell me their real issues? How am I earning trust?

Lesson Seven The Customer Is Not Always Right

Do I push back when a customer wants to do something that I am not sure helps them? Will I walk away from a sale?

Lesson Eight Above and Beyond Selling

Am I regularly doing things for customers that are way beyond what they are paying me for?

Lesson Nine Never Stop Learning

What is my commitment to learning? Does my use of time last week reflect what I say that commitment is?

Lesson Ten Refuse to Be a Commodity

It's not just about price. It's about value. How do I add prodigious amounts of value to reduce the ability to be a commodity?

Ultimately it comes down to three questions:

1. What am I going to do differently as a result of spending time with this book?

2. Which of the principles in this book do I need to be more consistent in using?

3. Are there things that are hurting my sales effectiveness that I need to stop doing?

The Magic of the 3 x 5 Cards

I've been sober over thirty-seven years. When I was newly sober, a friend saw that I was struggling with self-confidence. He gave me a book to read called *The Psychology of Winning* by Denis Waitley. Waitley was the Tony Robbins of the '80s, and his book generated over $100 million in sales. I read a chapter of that book almost every morning for at least two years, trying to take the principles he preached and make them part of my life.

The most powerful thing I learned from Waitley is captured in this line: "We are always moving in the direction of the things we think about most." Think things are going to be bad? They likely will be! Tell yourself that you always get a head cold in the summer or that you'll never make a certain amount of money, and guess what? You'll be right.

Waitley's book introduced me to the power of setting goals. A number of years later, Jack Canfield's book *The Success Principles* reinforced the power of setting goals. For years, I carried 3 x 5 cards around with me with each of my goals written on them. One goal per card. Why did I do that? To program my mind. I, like almost everyone, am a great forgetter. If you believe that Waitley is right and that we are moving in the direction of our thoughts, I need to program my thinking. And the 3 x 5 cards are the most effective way I have ever found to accomplish that.

I have written most of this book in the den of my home. Next to me as I write are a number of 3 x 5 cards. Today, my cards are less about how much money I want to have or some goal for our company. Today's cards more reflect the kind of husband, dad, or friend I aspire to be. But I go through them almost every day because that process reminds me of the person I want to be.

Nothing I have ever done has been more effective at moving me closer to my goals. Write down your goals, all of them, not just the business ones. Transfer them to 3 x 5 cards. And look at them frequently. That simple process will start you moving in the direction of those goals. And yes, it is that powerful.

All Change Is Incremental!

Do you know what screws up a lot of people? Setting overly ambitious goals that are almost impossible to achieve. If I say I want to lose fifty pounds, my brain will likely immediately think, *There is* no *way*. And it's pretty likely I will be eating pizza or a cheeseburger quickly. But if I have a goal of losing five pounds, that seems pretty achievable. I remember quoting Zig Ziglar once to one of my kids who was overwhelmed by home-work (What kind of dad does that?): "It's a cinch by the inch. It's hard by the yard." Simple, but brilliant.

What does "it's a cinch by the inch" mean as you work to incorporate the Servant Heart Selling lessons into your selling practice? It might mean that you would determine just one or two things that would have the maximum impact on your selling effectiveness. What are yours? Just work on them. The principle of focus is powerful. Work on fewer things and you increase the impact of the work you do. As it turns out, less really is more!

Few people change in straight line. Everyone experiences distractions, even setbacks, on the way to change. You have to be a little better before you can be a lot better. So focus on what incremental change looks like. If your goal is to ask better questions and become an acute listener, then prep for that on every sales call and take a few minutes after the call to review how you did. If you are like most of us, as you try to change, you will have some misses. But if you work at it consistently, you will change. And you will see the results.

Take Action

I've learned the hard way that perfectionism can be a form of procrastination. One of the most powerful success lessons of my life is the understanding that 80 percent of something imperfectly done is always better than 100 percent of something perfectly undone.

If this book has spoken to you, take action. Action is more powerful than thinking. Action is power.

One of my all-time favorite quotes from the great motivational speaker Les Brown sums it up for me: "To be successful, you must be willing to do the things today others won't do in order to have the things tomorrow others won't have."

WITH DEEP GRATITUDE

ALL OF US HAVE BEEN WARMED BY FIRES WE DID NOT
BUILD AND DRANK WATER FROM WELLS WE DID NOT DIG.
—SYNDICATED COLUMNIST MARK SHIELDS

I TRY TO SPEND SOME TIME EVERY SINGLE DAY THINKING
ABOUT THE THINGS I AM GRATEFUL FOR. Living in gratitude
is the foundation to creating a life of abundance.

As I wrap up the writing of this book, I am filled with gratitude and am especially grateful to all the people who have
helped shaped its message.

I am so grateful for all the companies that honored me with
the privilege of working with their teams in my time at JDA and
for the twenty-thousand-plus salespeople who have been part
of my seminars over the last thirty years. I have been blessed by
your energy and your desire to be better.

I think about the superstar sellers I've met in the media
business. I was supposed to be your teacher, but you turned out

to teach me. Your sales performance proved the principles that now make up this book. Thank you.

A bunch of very busy and very successful sellers and managers agreed to be interviewed for this book. Those discussions got me so excited and gave me so many good ideas. I hope this book makes you proud of the way you sell. You are truly my new heroes.

All the people I interviewed were referred to me by friends and business associates who instantly connected with this project when it was just a title and nothing further. Thanks to Mark Massepohl, Eric Meyrowitz, Ashley Gold, Dan Modisset, Pat Norris, Leon Long, Chester Elton, John Hannon, Cassie Doyle, and Bill Cates. Bill was the first person I called for ideas. He is himself a Servant Heart Seller, and he introduced me to my first two great interview subjects. Meg Linne, Rory Vaden, and Shamire Goodwin were great interviews themselves. And then they suggested others who became central to the message of this book. Thank you.

I have learned so much from the amazing people at JDA.media, formerly Jim Doyle and Associates. We say we are a company built on love, and I know I love and respect that group so much. I am especially grateful to our president and CEO, Angela Betasso. I spent over three years trying to persuade her to join JDA. And it has been the best sale I have ever made. She read an early draft and, as always, made it better.

I have a pet peeve about folks who say they are "self-made." I know without a doubt that without all the people, books, and seminars that have been my teacher, I would have accomplished very little. I am definitely not self-made. From first bosses to clients to mentors to spiritual advisers, I owe so much to so many.